Student Cookbook

Student Cookbook

OVER 100 EASY AND ECONOMICAL DISHES FOR HUNGRY STUDENTS

First published in 2010
LOVE FOOD is an imprint of Parragon Books Ltd

Parragon
Queen Street House
4 Queen Street
Bath BA1 1HE, UK

ISBN: 978-1-4454-0694-7

Printed in China

Design: Andrew Easton @ Ummagumma
Introduction (pages 6–7): Dominic Utton

With thanks to our student taste team: Laura Dickson, Lindsey Frost, Charlotte Hawken, Sophie Parker, Chemaine Shehadeh, Dan Toy, Anthony Trigo, and Fiona Wong

Notes for the Reader
This book uses imperial, metric, and US cup measurements. Follow the same units of measurement throughout; do not mix imperial and metric. All spoon measurements are level: teaspoons are assumed to be 5 ml, and tablespoons are assumed to be 15 ml. Unless otherwise stated, milk is assumed to be whole, eggs and individual vegetables, such as potatoes, are medium, and pepper is freshly ground black pepper.

The times given are an approximate guide only. Preparation times differ according to the techniques used by different people and the cooking times may also vary from those given as a result of the type of oven used. Optional ingredients, variations, or serving suggestions have not been included in the calculations.

Recipes using raw or very lightly cooked eggs should be avoided by infants, the elderly, pregnant women, convalescents, and anyone with a chronic condition. Pregnant and breastfeeding women are advised to avoid eating peanuts and peanut products. People with nut allergies should be aware that some of the prepared ingredients used in the recipes in this book may contain nuts. Always check the package before use. Vegetarians should be aware that some of the prepared ingredients used in the recipes in this book may contain animal products. Always check the package before use.

contents

introduction

So, you've finally done it. You've left home, struck out on your own. Congratulations: you've become a student. The hallowed halls of academia are calling and a wide world of learning beckons.

Well, something like that, anyway.

Going to college is not just about libraries, labs, and lectures—let's be honest, if it was, then the whole thing wouldn't be half as much fun. No: the real point of student life is what happens when you're away from your books. These years are about leaving the comforts (and restrictions) of home and experiencing stuff for yourself. There will be organizations to join, teams to get involved in. There's a (very) good chance the student union will become a place you're intimately familiar with. There will be an indecent number of parties, an embarrassing number of nights out. Over the next few years, you're going to have a better, more active, more exciting social life than you will ever experience again.

In short, you're going to have the time of your life.

Forget what they say about students having nothing better to do than sit around watching TV and surfing the internet: once you're in college you'll soon find that there are simply not enough hours in the day to cram it all in (even if that does include an afternoon nap). You're independent now—nobody's going to tell you what time to go to bed or what time to get up (though your professors might have some "suggestions" about this), nobody's going to dictate where and how often you go out...and nobody's going to tell you what to eat.

You do have some responsibilities, of course. Living on a budget is never easy, coping with doing your own laundry can take a bit of practice, and, given why you're there in the first place, some study may even have to be done. And, of course, with all the general craziness of student life, you're going to have to eat. Not only eat—you might have to cook. Once you reach college, the three square meals a day you had at home become a distant, impossible memory, and unless you learn your way around a kitchen, the sad result can be the kind of diet that would embarrass a dog.

It's tricky, we know. When you've got so much to do, taking the time out to prepare gourmet-quality meals can seem a pretty low priority. And when the pittance you're supposed to live on barely covers keeping you in haircuts and nights out, blowing your hard-earned cash on anything more nutritious than fast food can seem like pure wanton extravagance. But it needn't be so. There can be so much more to student cooking than ketchup pasta and box mac and cheese. A balanced diet does not mean equal parts cereal and milk. Putting together fresh, wholesome meals can be fast, easy, and, most importantly, cheap. And, crucially, it can involve a minimum of cleaning up afterward, too.

Learning to cook for yourself is not only healthier than a diet of takeouts and fast food, it's easier on the wallet, too. For the price of a couple of frozen dinners and a latte you can eat fresh food for a week. Getting stuck into the kitchen can be a great way to unwind at the end of the day, it can be a fantastic means of socializing with your fellow dorm mates and it's a pretty sure way to impress any potential dates. And, of course, knowing you're eating properly will give your parents one less thing to worry/nag about.

It really is easier than you think. Don't be intimidated. Yeah, so there's always going to be someone in your dorm who claims he can whip up a Béarnaise sauce quicker than you can crack a beer—like, whatever. As the recipes inside this book show, a repertoire of simple, wholesome, well-prepared meals is always going to be every bit as impressive as that fabulously complicated (and probably fictional) solitary cordon bleu creation he'll manage once a semester. With a little practice, you'll soon be making food that looks and smells so good you won't know whether to eat it or kiss it.

One last thing before you get busy with the pots and pans: remember that being able to put together a meal is just a part of student cooking. After all, being a student—whether you're living in dorms or living off campus—is about learning to live together. By all means show what you can do in the kitchen, but remember that it is a shared space. The last thing you want is fights over fridge space and oven rights. Everyone's heard the stories of stolen eggs, watered-down orange juice, people spiking each other's bread with salt...and of course there's the now infamous note left on one shared student fridge: "Keep out," it read, "I lick my cheese." You don't want to have to be reading that first thing in the morning!

The student kitchen can be so much more than a place to boil water or scrounge some toast: it can be the center of your home life. Cooking for your roommates will forge strong bonds—and should make sure you get a few free meals back, too. And most of all, it's fun! So grab an apron and get started. Trust us: there's really nothing like a bit of home cooking for finally shaking that 14-hour hangover...

shopping

If you want to whip up a storm in the kitchen, you're going to have to hit the stores first. Find what works for you—you may prefer to shop for a few things each day, make a weekly grocery trip, or save up for a monthly supermarket sweep. Alternatively, you could avoid the supermarket altogether and shop at the market. Whatever you decide to do, the following tips should help you to make the most of your finances.

1. Set a budget: Work out how much you can afford to spend on food (remembering to factor in the occasional late-night fast food or delivery) and stick to it. You may want to have a separate budget for alcohol!

2. Plan your meals: Making a menu plan for the week ahead and only buying what you actually need (rather than what you think you need) is one of the easiest ways to cut your food bill. It doesn't have to be too restrictive either—you can juggle the meals around during the week depending on what you feel like eating.

3. Write a list: There's nothing worse than getting home and realizing that you've forgotten to buy a vital ingredient. Having a list will also stop you from making those impulse purchases that bump up your shopping bill. Take a pen and check off the items as you put them in your basket.

4. Check your stock: Before you go shopping, have a quick rummage through your cabinets. You never know what hidden gems you might find in there, plus there's no point in buying something that you already have. Look in the fridge and throw away anything that's spoiled to make room for your new purchases.

5. Don't shop for food on an empty stomach: This is a definite no-no for anyone on a budget because you'll be much more likely to give in to temptation and buy things that aren't on your list if your stomach is growling.

6. Give yourself enough time to shop: If you're in a rush, you're much more likely to end up panic buying and reaching for the first thing you see, rather than considering which items are the best value. Take a few moments to compare similar products and always check the expiration dates on perishable items.

7. Don't buy everything at once: Don't rush out and buy every item on the staples list (see page 10) right away. Start with a few basics and build up your supplies as you try new recipes. There's no point buying a load of spices if you never cook anything more adventurous than pasta and sauce! Similarly, if an ingredient is new to you, buy a small package to see if you like it before you stock up.

8. Don't be put off trying supermarket-brand products: Just because your family buys the premium version of a product, doesn't mean that you should! Branded foods might seem familiar, but the reality is that the economy equivalent is more suited to the student wallet. Besides, we figure you won't be able to taste the difference anyway.

9. Don't buy more than you need: Super-size packs aren't such a good deal if you end up throwing half of their contents away because they're spoiled before you have the chance to finish them! If you are buying in bulk, consider getting together with a few friends so you can split the cost, or stick to nonperishable items that you know you will use.

10. Be a coupon queen or king: When you're flicking through magazines or newspapers, keep an eye out for money-off coupons. Cut out any for products that you usually buy and safely stash them in your wallet until your next shopping trip.

11. Make friends with your freezer: It's not just there for vodka and frozen dinners! Frozen vegetables are just as nutritious as fresh ones and fresh sliced bread can be frozen and taken out a slice at a time as you need it. You can also freeze any leftover soups and casseroles to eat another day.

12. Buy loose fruit and vegetables: They tend to be cheaper than prepacked ones. Also, because you only have to buy as many as you actually need, you're less likely to discover rotting vegetables in your cabinet a few weeks along the line.

13. Consider internet shopping: Most supermarkets offer an online order and delivery service for groceries. It's especially useful if you don't have a car as you can order bulky or heavy items that you wouldn't be able to lug home yourself. There's usually a small delivery fee but you could always do a joint shop with some of your fellow students and share the cost. Online shopping is also good if you're prone to making impulse

purchases while wandering around the supermarket—if it's out of sight, it's out of mind!

14. Preparation is key: Convenience foods, such as sliced mushrooms and grated cheese, may save time and hassle in the kitchen but at considerable cost. If you can spare a few extra minutes to prepare ingredients yourself, you'll make significant savings.

15. Don't get stuck in a rut: It's easy to get into the habit of eating the same foods week in, week out. Banish boredom by varying your meals—the recipes in this book should certainly provide plenty of inspiration!

the staples

The list below gives a number of basic pantry items that are useful to get you started. As you work through the recipes in this book, you'll quickly build up a stash of ingredients and, after a while, you'll find that you already have many of the items you need to try a new recipe.

Cans and jars
Tomatoes
Beans, such as cannellini beans, kidney beans, and black beans
Fish, such as tuna, salmon, and sardines
Honey
Peanut butter

Bottles
Vegetable or peanut oil
Olive oil

Condiments
Salt
Pepper
Dried herbs, such as oregano, thyme, and bay leaves

Dried spices, such as ground coriander, cumin, paprika, and cinnamon
Dried chile flakes
Curry powder/paste
Ketchup
Soy sauce
Worcestershire sauce
Mustard
Vinegar

Dry goods
Flour
Oats
Sugar
Bouillon cubes
Pasta
Noodles
Rice
Cereal

Fresh
Milk
Butter/margarine
Cheese
Eggs

Frozen
Fruit and vegetables, such as frozen berries, peas, and corn
Bread

Other supplies
Paper towels
Plastic wrap/sandwich bags
Aluminum foil
Garbage bags
Cleaning products

clean & tidy

Okay, so your average student kitchen is unlikely to be a haven of hygiene but it doesn't have to be a grotto of grime either! Cleaning doesn't have to be a chore if you keep on top of it. The tips below should point you in the right direction and help you to avoid a nasty bout of food poisoning.

- Wipe down the surfaces before and after cooking using a clean sponge or cloth.

- Sweep the floor regularly—unless you want to share your kitchen with rodents and cockroaches!

- Wipe up any spills on the stove top after use. It's much easier to clean them off right away rather than leaving them until they're practically welded on.

- Avoid arguments by organizing a cleaning rotation so that one person doesn't end up rushing around cleaning up after everybody.

- Wash your hands regularly before and during cooking, especially if you've been handling raw meat and poultry. Dry them on a clean towel—not one you found in a heap on the floor!

- Check your fridge temperature—it should be below 41°F/5°C in order to keep your food nicely chilled.

- Clear out the fridge regularly and throw away anything that's past its best. You don't want to be pouring sour, lumpy milk onto your breakfast cereal!

- Keep cooked and raw foods separate in the fridge. Ideally, raw meat, poultry, and fish should be stored on the bottom shelf so it can't drip onto any food underneath.

- Leftovers should be cooled first, then stored in the fridge in airtight containers.

- Do not refreeze foods that have already been frozen and thawed.

kitchen safety

Kitchens can be really dangerous places, and the student kitchen is no exception. With hazards including sharp knives, boiling water, electrical appliances, and hot surfaces, not to mention the fact that it's populated by a rowdy group of novice cooks, it's probably the deadliest room in the entire house! But don't be alarmed—by following the tips below you can minimize the risks to yourself and others.

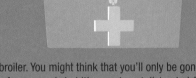

- Mop up any spills before someone slips on them.

- Always use (dry) oven mitts to handle hot pans or dishes.

- Carry knives by your side with the tip pointing downward.

- Don't leave sharp items, such as knives, in a sink full of water. The next person to put their hand in there might get a nasty surprise!

- If you're using the stove top, make sure that your pan handle is positioned to the side, rather than the front, so that it can't easily be knocked off.

- Don't place flammable items, such as dish towels, close to the stove top.

- Broiler pans full of accumulated fat are a potential fire hazard, as well as being disgusting! By lining the pan with aluminum foil and removing and discarding after each use, you'll never have to face the chore of cleaning a dirty broiler pan again. Do not line the broiler rack as this will stop the fat from draining off and may cause flare ups.

- Don't wander off while you're cooking, leaving a hot pan on the stove top or anything under the broiler. You might think that you'll only be gone for a few seconds but it's easy to get distracted. This is especially important if you're cooking with oil, as the pan can easily catch fire.

- If a pan does catch fire, do not attempt to move it but do turn off the heat if it's safe to do so (i.e. if you don't have to lean over the pan to reach the controls). Cover with a fire blanket or damp dish towel and leave until cool. Never throw water over a pan fire or use a fire extinguisher.

- If an electrical appliance is on fire, pull out the plug if it's safe to do so, or switch off at the fusebox. If this doesn't stop the fire, try to smother it with a fire blanket or use a carbon dioxide extinguisher.

- If you can't deal with a fire yourself, leave the kitchen, closing the door behind you, and call 911. Make sure that others are aware of the fire (break the glass on the fire alarm if there is one) and evacuate the building.

about this book

Further hints and tips give useful advice and offer guidance to the beginner cook.

Number of servings. Most recipes can easily be halved or doubled, depending on how many people you've got to feed.

These symbols give at-a-glance information about the recipe, such as whether it is suitable for vegetarians. For further information, see the key below.

Each recipe includes a full list of ingredients, with preparation instructions where necessary. Assemble all your ingredients before you start cooking.

pasta salad

Serves 2

Ingredients
3½ oz/100 g dried pasta spirals
2 tbsp olive oil, plus extra if needed
1 tbsp mayonnaise
1 tbsp plain yogurt
2 tbsp pesto
7 oz/200 g canned tuna, drained
  and flaked
7 oz/200 g canned corn kernels, drained
2 tomatoes, peeled, seeded, and chopped
½ green bell pepper, seeded and chopped
½ avocado, pitted, peeled, and chopped
salt and pepper

Pasta salads are incredibly versatile—just add any salad ingredients you have to hand. Vegetarians could use drained canned beans in place of the tuna.

Method
1 Bring a large pan of lightly salted water to a boil. Add the pasta, return to a boil, and cook for 8–10 minutes, until tender but still firm to the bite. Drain, return to the pan, and add the oil. Toss well to coat, then cover and let cool.
2 Whisk the mayonnaise, yogurt, and pesto together in a pitcher, adding a little oil if needed to achieve the desired consistency. Add a pinch of salt and season to taste with pepper.
3 Mix the cooled pasta with the tuna, corn, tomatoes, bell pepper, and avocado, add the dressing, and toss well to coat. Serve immediately or transfer to an airtight container for a brown bag lunch.

STUDENT TASTE TEAM
Name: Dan Toy
Studying: Writing for Publication, Performance and Media
At: Pratt Institute, NY USA
Marks: 9/10
Comments about dish: This recipe necessitated inexpensive ingredients and was easy to make

62

KEY

Healthy

Veggie

Speedy

Cheap

Impressive

One pot

Spicy

Some of the recipes have been tested by our specially selected student taste team. You'll find their comments (and marks out of ten!) here.

All the recipes feature step-by-step instructions, making them easy to follow—even for novice cooks! Always read through the recipe before you start, noting the timings and the equipment needed.

All the recipes are accompanied by a color photograph of the finished dish

13

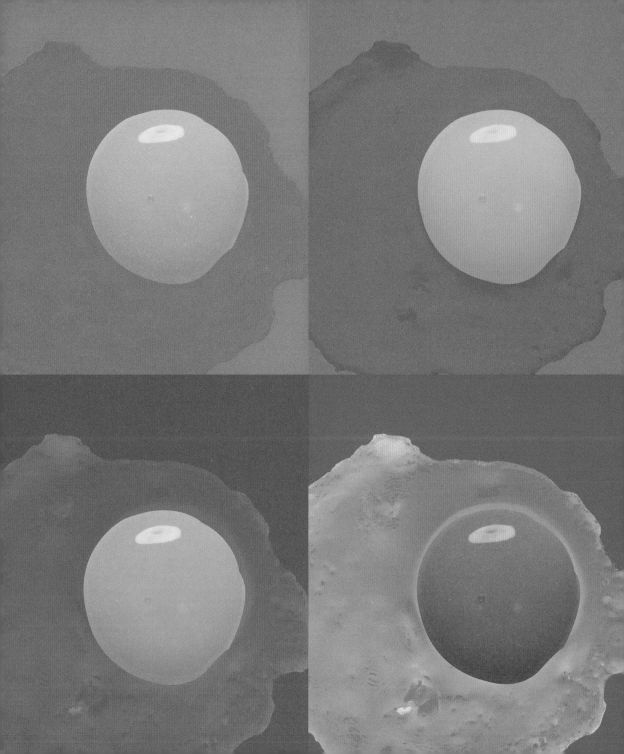

the big breakfast

It's tempting to skip breakfast in favor of extra snoozing time, but eating a hearty breakfast really is the best start to the day. It's the perfect opportunity to fuel up ready for a hectic day's studying, especially if you're not sure if you'll get a chance to stop for lunch. Whether you're after a recipe for a quick weekday breakfast or a lazy Sunday brunch, this chapter contains all sorts of tempting treats to entice you out from under the blankets.

fruity yogurt with granola

Serves 1

Ingredients
2⅓ cups rolled oats
2 tbsp honey
2 tbsp pumpkin seeds
2 tbsp sunflower seeds
2 tbsp chopped walnuts
1 small ripe pear, peeled,
     cored, and chopped
½ ripe mango, pitted, peeled, and chopped
generous ½ cup plain yogurt

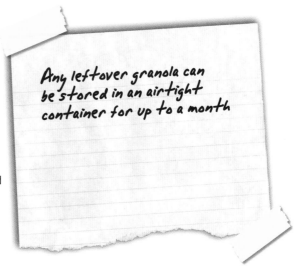

Any leftover granola can be stored in an airtight container for up to a month

Method
1 Preheat the oven to 350°F/180°C.

2 For the granola, mix the oats and honey together in a bowl and spread out on a baking sheet. Bake in the preheated oven for 10–15 minutes, stirring a couple of times, until the oats are lightly browned, then remove from the oven and let cool.

3 Place the seeds in a bowl and briefly grind with the end of a rolling pin to break them into smaller pieces. Mix with the cooled oats and the walnuts.

4 To assemble, put half the pear and mango in a glass and top with half the yogurt and a spoonful of granola. Repeat with the remaining fruit and yogurt and top with more granola.

fruity oatmeal

Serves 4

Ingredients

2 cups rolled oats

generous ½ cup oatmeal

pinch of salt (optional)

3½ cups milk

⅓ cup plumped dried apricots, chopped

2 tbsp sunflower seeds

2 bananas, peeled and sliced

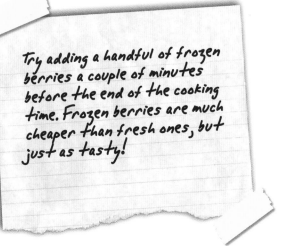

Try adding a handful of frozen berries a couple of minutes before the end of the cooking time. Frozen berries are much cheaper than fresh ones, but just as tasty!

Method

1 Place the oats and oatmeal in a pan together with the salt, if using, and stir in the milk. Place over low heat and cook, stirring, for 7–8 minutes, or until the oats thicken.

2 Stir the apricots and sunflower seeds into the pan, then spoon into individual dishes and top with the sliced banana.

citrus zinger

Serves 1

Ingredients

1 pink grapefruit

1 orange

½ lemon

½ lime

lime slice, to decorate

Method

1 Cut the grapefruit and orange in half using a sharp knife.

2 Using a lemon squeezer, juice the grapefruit, orange, lemon, and lime and pour into a glass. Stir, decorate with a lime slice and serve immediately.

banana breakfast shake

Serves 2

Ingredients

2 ripe bananas, peeled and chopped

¾ cup plain yogurt

½ cup milk

½ tsp vanilla extract

honey, for drizzling

Method

1 Put the bananas, yogurt, milk, and vanilla extract into a tall beaker.

2 Using a handheld stick blender, process until smooth.

3 Pour into glasses, drizzle with honey, and serve immediately.

blueberry bliss

Serves 2

Ingredients

1⅓ cups fresh or frozen blueberries
2¼ cups vanilla-flavored yogurt
½ large banana, peeled and chopped
lemon juice or honey, to taste

Method

1 Put the blueberries, yogurt, and banana into a tall beaker.

2 Using a handheld stick blender, process until smooth.

3 Add a little lemon juice or honey to taste, then process again. Pour into glasses and serve immediately.

mango smoothie

Serves 1

Ingredients

1 mango, peeled, pitted, and sliced
1 tsp honey
scant 1 cup orange juice
2 tbsp plain yogurt

Method

1 Put the mango, honey, orange juice, and yogurt into a tall beaker.

2 Using a handheld stick blender, process until smooth.

3 Pour into a glass and serve immediately.

melon & strawberry crunch

Serves 4

Ingredients

⅓ cup rolled oats

¼ cup oat bran

2 tbsp toasted slivered almonds

scant ¼ cup plumped dried apricots, finely chopped

½ melon, such as galia

1¼ cups strawberries, hulled

⅔ cup orange juice or milk, to serve (optional)

Method

1 Put the rolled oats and oat bran in a bowl and stir in the almonds and dried apricots.

2 Discard the skin and seeds from the melon and cut into small bite-size pieces. Halve the strawberries if large.

3 Divide the rolled oat mixture among 4 individual bowls, then top with the melon and strawberries. If liked, serve with either orange juice or milk.

broiled cinnamon oranges

Serves 6

Ingredients

3 large oranges

1 tsp ground cinnamon

1 tbsp raw brown sugar

Method

1 Preheat the broiler to high. Cut the oranges in half and discard any pips. Using a sharp knife or a curved grapefruit knife, carefully cut the flesh away from the skin by cutting around the edge of the fruit. Cut across the segments to loosen the flesh into bite-size pieces that will then spoon out easily.

2 Arrange the orange halves, cut-side up, in a shallow, ovenproof dish. Mix the cinnamon with the sugar in a small bowl and sprinkle evenly over the orange halves.

3 Cook under the preheated broiler for 3–5 minutes, or until the sugar has caramelized and is golden and bubbling. Serve immediately.

Most fruits are available year-round but bear in mind that they will be cheaper when they're in season.

baked croissants with peaches

Serves 4

Ingredients

6–8 stale croissants

10½ oz/300 g canned peaches in juice

generous 2 cups milk

3 eggs

6 tbsp granulated sugar

confectioners' sugar, for dusting (optional)

This dish is perfect for a lazy weekend brunch. Try using different canned fruits in place of the peaches.

Method

1 Preheat the oven to 375°F/190°C.

2 Halve the croissants and put them into a baking dish in layers. Drain the peaches, reserving the juice. Cut the peaches into pieces and scatter over the croissants.

3 Put the milk, eggs, and 4 tablespoons of the granulated sugar into a pitcher and beat well. Pour slowly and evenly over the croissants, then let stand for 5 minutes, pressing the croissants into the milk from time to time, so that the croissants soak up the liquid.

4 Sprinkle over the remaining granulated sugar, then bake in the preheated oven for 25 minutes, until risen and golden.

5 Dust with confectioners' sugar, if using. Spoon onto plates and drizzle over a little of the reserved peach juice from the can.

sweet scrambled eggs with cornflakes

Serves 1

Ingredients

2 large eggs

2 tbsp granulated sugar,
plus extra for sprinkling

1½ cups cornflakes

1 tbsp butter

pinch of ground cinnamon

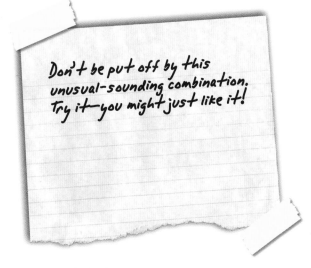

Don't be put off by this unusual-sounding combination. Try it—you might just like it!

Method

1 Beat the eggs and sugar together in a bowl. Quickly mix in the cornflakes so that they do not soften too much.

2 Melt the butter in a skillet until it foams, then pour in the egg-and-cornflake mixture. Cook, stirring, until the egg has set softly.

3 Spoon onto a plate and sprinkle over the cinnamon and a little extra sugar. Serve immediately.

french toast

Serves 2

Ingredients

2 slices stale white bread

scant ½ cup milk

1 egg

pinch of salt

2 tbsp unsalted butter

½ tsp ground cinnamon

1 tsp granulated sugar

Method

1 Slice the bread in half diagonally and place, in a single layer, in a shallow dish. Pour over the milk and let soak for 1–2 minutes, then turn over the bread.

2 Place the egg and salt in a bowl and beat well. Dip the soaked bread slices into the egg mix.

3 Heat the butter in a skillet until it foams, then add the bread slices. Cook the French toast until golden brown on both sides. Drain on paper towels, then transfer to serving plates.

4 Mix together the cinnamon and sugar in a small bowl, then sprinkle over the French toast. Serve immediately.

cinnamon apples on fruit toast

Serves 1

Ingredients

1 tbsp butter

½ tsp ground cinnamon

1 apple, cored and sliced

1 slice fruit bread

corn syrup, to serve

Method

1 Melt the butter in a pan over low heat and stir in the cinnamon. Add the apple and stir well to coat.

2 Preheat the broiler and line the broiler pan with foil. Spread the buttered apple over the broiler pan. Cook under the preheated broiler until the apple is just beginning to brown.

3 Toast the fruit bread in a toaster or under the broiler. Serve the toast with the apples piled on top, drizzled with a little corn syrup.

Fruity toast toppings make a tasty alternative to jelly. A firm pear would work equally well in place of the apple.

apple pancakes with maple syrup butter

Serves 4–6

Ingredients
scant 1½ cups self-rising flour
½ cup superfine sugar
1 tsp ground cinnamon
1 egg
scant 1 cup milk
2 apples, peeled and grated
1 tsp butter
apple wedges, to serve

Maple syrup butter
6 tbsp softened butter
3 tbsp maple syrup

These pancakes are the perfect breakfast when you've got friends over to stay or if you want a pancake party! If your budget doesn't quite stretch to maple syrup, substitute corn syrup.

Method

1 Mix the flour, sugar and cinnamon together in a bowl and make a well in the center. Beat the egg and the milk together and pour into the well. Using a wooden spoon, gently incorporate the dry ingredients into the liquid until well combined, then stir in the grated apple.

2 Heat the butter in a large, nonstick skillet over low heat until melted and bubbling. Add tablespoons of the batter to form 3½-inch/9-cm circles. Cook each pancake for about 1 minute, until it starts to bubble lightly on the top and looks set, then flip it over and cook the other side for 30 seconds, or until cooked through. The pancakes should be golden brown; if not, increase the heat a little. Remove from the skillet and keep warm. Repeat the process until all of the batter has been used up (it is not necessary to add extra butter to the skillet).

3 To make the maple syrup butter, melt the 6 tablespoons of butter with the maple syrup in a saucepan over low heat and stir until combined. To serve, place the pancakes on serving dishes and spoon over the flavored butter. Serve with apple wedges.

fruity muffins

Makes 10

Ingredients

2 cups self-rising whole wheat flour

2 tsp baking powder

2 tbsp dark brown sugar

generous ½ cup plumped dried apricots, finely chopped

1 banana, peeled and mashed with 1 tbsp orange juice

1 tsp finely grated orange rind

1¼ cups milk

1 large egg, beaten

3 tbsp sunflower oil

2 tbsp rolled oats

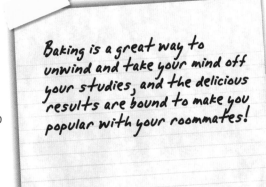

Baking is a great way to unwind and take your mind off your studies, and the delicious results are bound to make you popular with your roommates!

Method

1 Preheat the oven to 400°F/200°C. Line 10 cups of a 12-cup muffin pan with muffin paper liners. Sift the flour and baking powder into a mixing bowl, adding any husks that remain in the strainer. Stir in the sugar and chopped apricots.

2 Make a well in the center and add the mashed banana, orange rind, milk, egg, and oil. Stir gently until just combined; do not overmix. Divide evenly among the paper liners.

3 Sprinkle over the oats and bake in the preheated oven for 25–30 minutes, until well risen and firm to the touch, or until a toothpick inserted into the center comes out clean.

4 Remove the muffins from the oven and place them on a wire rack to cool slightly. Serve the muffins while still warm.

STUDENT TASTE TEAM

Name: Sophie Parker

Studying: Bachelor of Law

At: University of Otago, New Zealand

Comments about dish: Great for a cold morning or a weekend brunch—yum!

Marks:

7.5/10

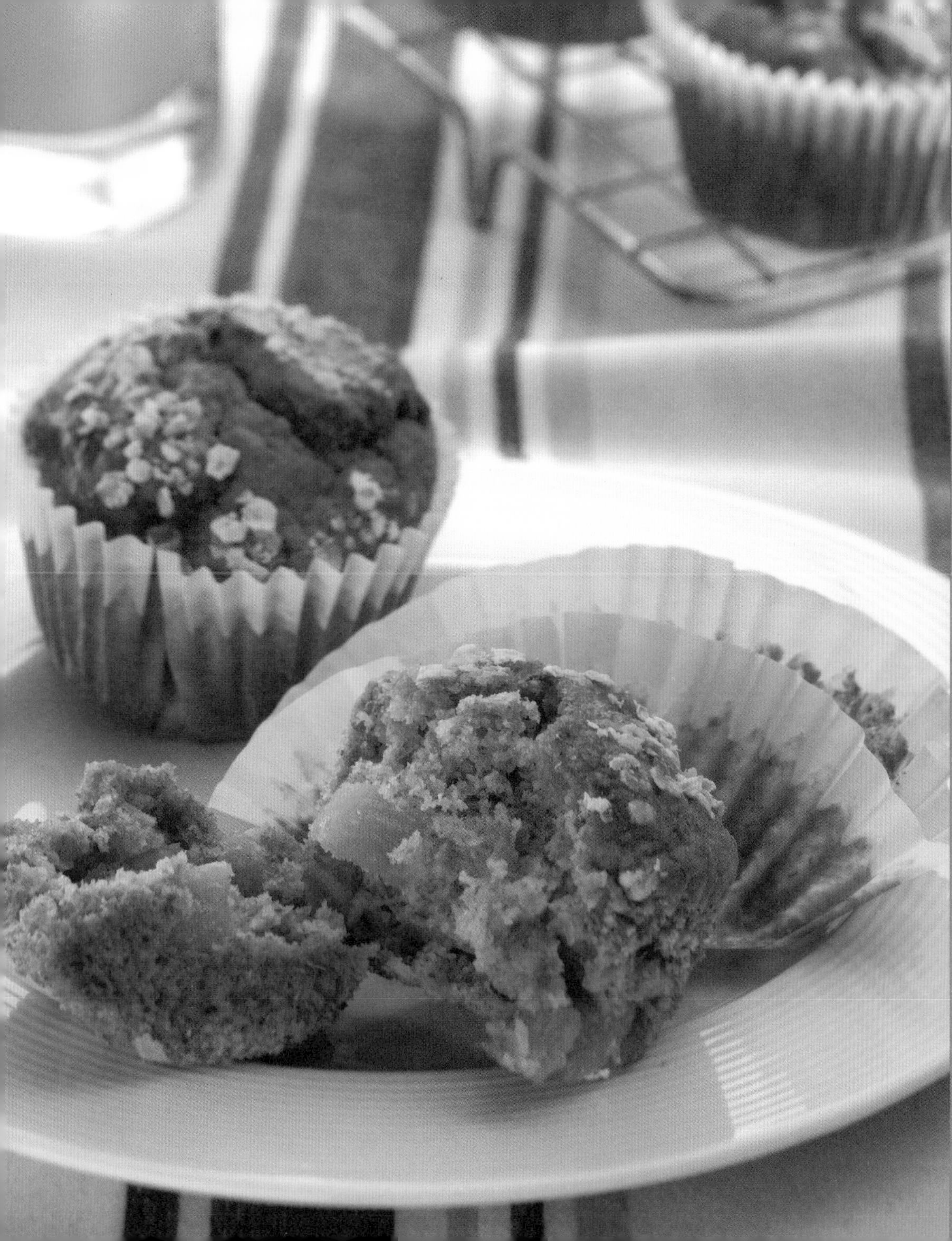

ham & cheese croissant

Serves 1

Ingredients

1 croissant

1 egg, hard-cooked and sliced (optional)

2 thin slices cooked ham, halved

mustard, to taste (optional)

2 slices hard cheese, such as cheddar, Gruyère, or Emmental

Method

1 Preheat the broiler to medium–high. Slice the croissant horizontally in half, then lay it, cut-sides up, on the rack in the broiler pan.

2 Top each croissant half with half the hard-cooked egg, if using, and a slice of ham, and spread with a little mustard, if using. Top with the cheese, cutting and overlapping the slices to fit the croissant. Cook under the preheated broiler for about 2 minutes, until the cheese has melted. The croissant will be warmed through and beginning to brown around the edges.

3 Invert the top half of the croissant on top of the bottom half. Serve immediately.

chive scrambled eggs

Serves 2

Ingredients

4 eggs

⅓ cup light cream

2 tbsp snipped fresh chives, plus extra to garnish

2 tbsp butter

4 slices bread

salt and pepper

Method

1 Break the eggs into a bowl and whisk gently with the cream. Season to taste with salt and pepper and add the snipped chives.

2 Melt the butter in a skillet and pour in the egg mixture. Let set slightly, then move the mixture toward the center of the skillet using a wooden spoon as the eggs start to cook. Continue in this way until the eggs are cooked but still creamy.

3 Lightly toast the bread in a toaster or under a preheated broiler and place on serving plates. Spoon over the scrambled eggs and serve immediately, garnished with chives.

For a hard-cooked egg, cook the egg in a pan of simmering water for 8 minutes.

sunshine toast

Serves 1

Ingredients

1 slice whole wheat bread

1 tbsp corn oil

2–3 mushrooms, sliced

1 tomato, halved

1 small egg

pepper

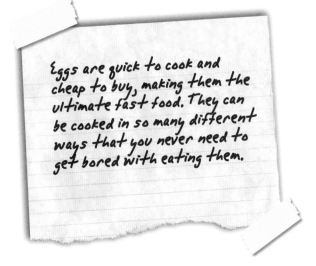

Eggs are quick to cook and cheap to buy, making them the ultimate fast food. They can be cooked in so many different ways that you never need to get bored with eating them.

Method

1 Lightly toast the bread in a toaster or under a preheated broiler. Using a cookie cutter, cut a hole in the center of the slice of toast, large enough to hold the egg.

2 Heat the oil in a nonstick skillet and cook the mushrooms and tomato, cut-sides down, for 3–4 minutes, until the mushrooms are beginning to brown. Turn the tomato over.

3 Make a space in the middle of the skillet and add the toast. Crack the egg open and carefully pour it into the hole in the toast. Reduce the heat and cook slowly until cooked through.

4 Season to taste with pepper, then transfer to a serving plate.

potato cakes with bacon & eggs

Serves 4

Ingredients

1 lb/450g potatoes, peeled

5 eggs

3 tbsp all-purpose flour

3 tbsp corn oil

8 slices bacon

6 cherry tomatoes, halved

salt and pepper

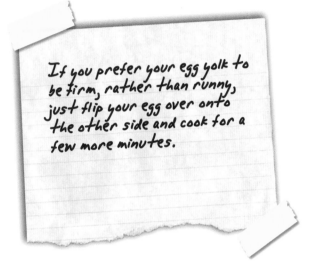

If you prefer your egg yolk to be firm, rather than runny, just flip your egg over onto the other side and cook for a few more minutes.

Method

1 Preheat the broiler to medium–high.

2 Grate the potatoes, rinse in a strainer, then spread out on a clean dish towel. Gather up the sides and squeeze to remove any water.

3 Beat 1 of the eggs in a large bowl. Add the potatoes, flour, and salt and pepper to taste and stir well. Take handfuls of the potato mixture and form into round patties about 2¾ inches/7 cm across. Heat 2 tablespoons of the oil in a skillet. Cook the potato cakes, in batches, for 5 minutes on each side, until golden. Drain on paper towels.

4 Place the bacon on the broiler rack and cook under the preheated broiler for 8 minutes, turning once, until crisp. Broil the tomatoes for 2–3 minutes.

5 Meanwhile, add the remaining oil to the skillet and fry the remaining eggs for 5 minutes, until the whites are set.

6 Transfer the potato cakes, bacon, tomatoes, and eggs to plates and serve immediately.

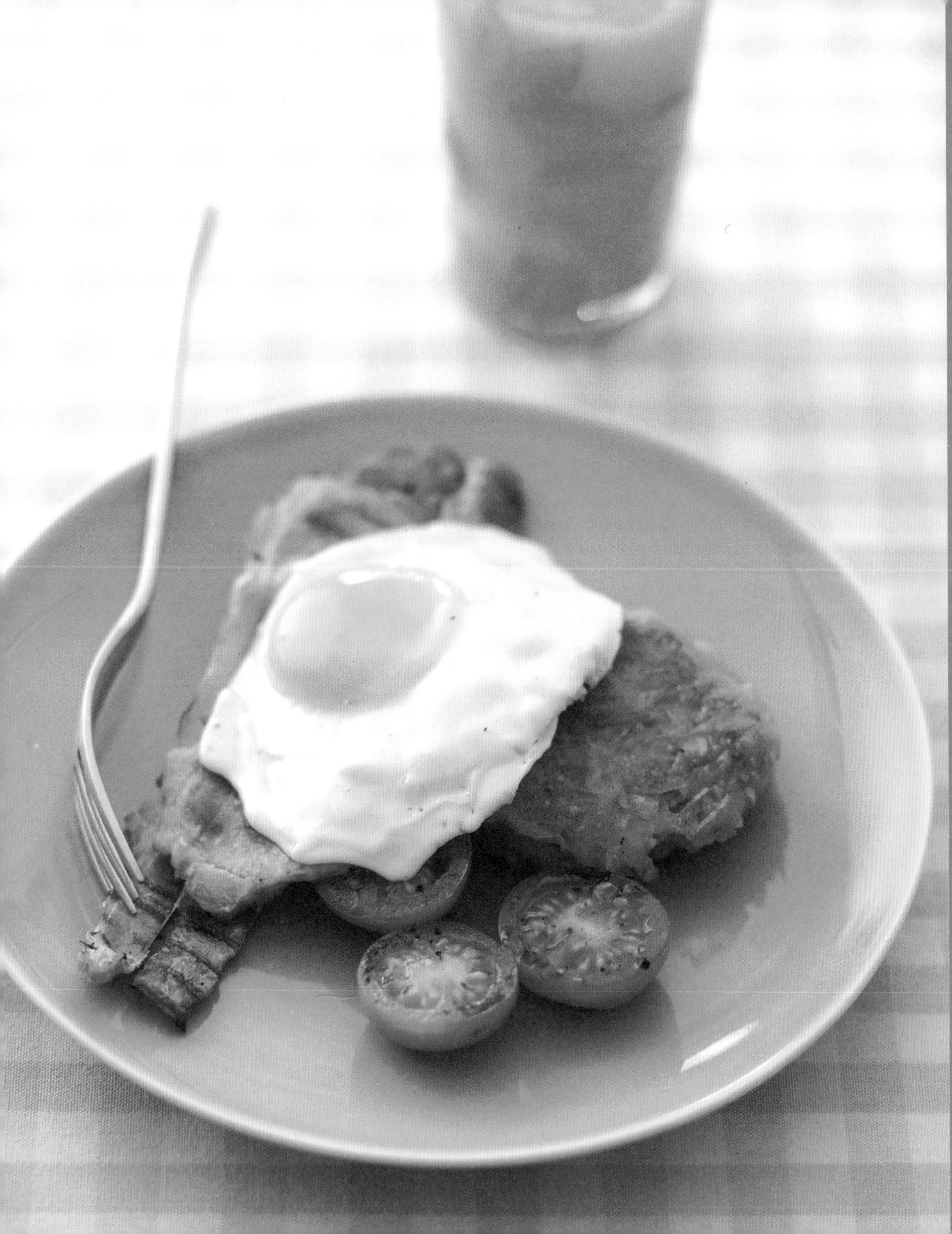

breakfast omelet

Serves 4

Ingredients

4 pork or vegetarian sausages

pat of butter

2 tsp corn oil, plus extra if necessary

12 cherry tomatoes

6 eggs, beaten

salt and pepper

Method

1 Preheat the broiler to medium–high. Line the broiler pan with foil. Arrange the sausages on the broiler rack and cook under the preheated broiler, turning frequently, until cooked through and golden all over. Let cool slightly, then cut into bite-size pieces.

2 Meanwhile, melt the butter with the oil in a skillet with a heatproof handle and cook the tomatoes, turning occasionally, for 2 minutes.

3 Add the sausage pieces so that they are evenly distributed in the bottom of the skillet among the tomatoes. Add a little more oil if the skillet appears dry.

4 Season the eggs to taste with salt and pepper and pour over the sausages and tomatoes. Cook for 3 minutes, without stirring, then place the skillet under the broiler and cook the top for 3 minutes, or until set and lightly golden. Cut into wedges to serve.

baked eggs with ham & tomato

Serves 1

Ingredients

1 tsp olive oil

½ small leek, chopped

2 thin slices cooked ham, chopped

1 egg

¼ cup grated cheddar cheese

2 slices tomato

Method

1 Preheat the oven to 350°F/180°C. Heat the oil in a pan and cook the leek for 5–6 minutes, until soft.

2 Place the leek in the bottom of a ramekin and top with the ham. Crack and pour in the egg, then top with the cheese and tomato.

3 Bake in the preheated oven for 10 minutes, until the egg is set. Remove the ramekin from the oven, let cool a little, and serve.

To test whether an egg is fresh, place it in a bowl of water—generally, a stale egg will float.

eggs benedict

Serves 4

Ingredients
1 tbsp white wine vinegar
4 eggs
4 English muffins
4 slices cooked ham

Quick hollandaise sauce
3 egg yolks
scant 1 cup butter
1 tbsp lemon juice
pepper

If you haven't got a blender or food processor, place the egg yolks in a heatproof bowl set over a pan of gently simmering water and gradually add the melted butter, beating constantly with a wire whisk.

Method

1 To poach an egg, fill a pan three-quarters full with water and bring to a boil over low heat. Reduce the heat to a simmer and add the vinegar. When the water is barely simmering, carefully break the egg into the pan. Poach the egg for 3 minutes, or until the white is just set but the yolk is still soft. Remove with a slotted spoon and drain on paper towels. Repeat with the remaining eggs.

2 Meanwhile, to make the hollandaise sauce, place the egg yolks in a blender or food processor. Melt the butter in a small pan until bubbling. With the motor running, gradually add the hot butter to the blender in a steady stream until the sauce is thick and creamy. Add the lemon juice, and a little warm water if the sauce is too thick, then season to taste with pepper. Remove from the blender and keep warm.

3 Split the muffins and toast them on both sides in a toaster or under a preheated broiler. To serve, top each muffin with a slice of ham, a poached egg, and a generous spoonful of hollandaise sauce.

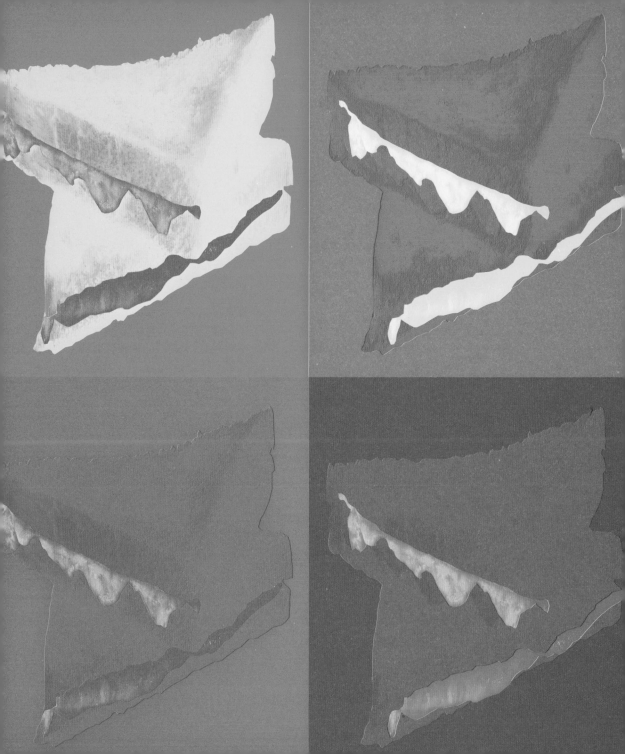

grab and go

The cost of buying lunch each day—even if it's only from a student cafeteria—can soon mount up. It might sound boring, but making your own is a great way to save cash. With plenty of inspiring ideas to choose from—including soups, salads, and sweet treats—the recipes in this chapter prove that there is more to lunch than soggy sandwiches. Just prepare the night before and in the morning you can just grab…and go!

simply super sandwich fillings

Serves 2

Ingredients
Crunchy tuna
7 oz/200 g canned tuna, drained and flaked

1 tbsp canned corn kernels, drained

1 tbsp chopped bell peppers

1 tbsp mayonnaise

Fruity cheese spread
½ cup low-fat cream cheese

1 tbsp chopped pitted dates

2 tbsp chopped plumped dried apricots

Chicken & avocado
½ chicken breast, cooked and finely chopped

½ small avocado, mashed with 2 tsp lemon juice

Making your own sandwiches is an easy way to save cash, but you'll quickly get bored with them if you have the same filling each day. Try these original ideas when you're short of inspiration.

Method
1 Mix the ingredients for each filling together and store in an airtight container in the refrigerator until required.

tex-mex roll-ups

Serves 2

Ingredients

2 corn tortillas

2 tbsp refried beans

2 tbsp grated cheddar cheese

2–3 tbsp finely chopped cooked chicken

1 tomato, sliced

¼ avocado, peeled, pitted, and cut into strips

Method

1 Put each tortilla on a microwavable plate. Spread the beans over the tortillas and sprinkle with the cheese. Microwave for about 15 seconds, until the cheese melts. Let cool slightly.

2 Arrange the chicken, tomato, and avocado on top. Roll up and cut into small pieces. Wrap in foil for a brown bag lunch.

tortillas with tuna, egg & corn

Serves 2

Ingredients

1 tbsp plain yogurt

1 tsp olive oil

½ tsp white wine vinegar

½ tsp Dijon mustard

1 large egg, hard-cooked and cooled

7 oz/200 g canned tuna, drained

7 oz/200 g canned corn kernels, drained

2 flour tortillas

1 container mustard and cress

pepper

Method

1 To make the dressing, whisk the yogurt, oil, vinegar, mustard, and pepper to taste in a pitcher until emulsified and smooth.

2 Shell the egg, separate the yolk and the white, then mash the yolk and finely chop the white. Mash the tuna with the egg and dressing, then mix in the corn.

3 Spread the filling equally over the tortillas and sprinkle over the mustard and cress. Fold in one end and roll up. Wrap in foil for a brown bag lunch.

chicken wraps

Serves 4

Ingredients

⅔ cup plain yogurt

1 tbsp whole grain mustard

1 large skinless, boneless chicken breast, cooked and diced

2 cups shredded Iceberg lettuce

2¾-inch/7-cm piece cucumber, thinly sliced

2 celery stalks, sliced

½ cup black seedless grapes, halved

4 flour tortillas

pepper

Method

1 Combine the yogurt and mustard in a bowl and season to taste with pepper. Stir in the chicken and toss until thoroughly coated.

2 Put the lettuce, cucumber, celery, and grapes into a separate bowl and mix well.

3 Fold a tortilla in half and in half again to make a cone that is easy to hold. Half-fill the tortilla pocket with the salad mixture and top with some of the chicken mixture. Repeat with the remaining tortillas, salad, and chicken. Wrap in foil for a brown bag lunch.

turkey salad pita

Serves 1

Ingredients

small handful of baby spinach, rinsed, patted dry, and shredded

½ red bell pepper, seeded and thinly sliced

½ carrot, peeled and coarsely grated

4 tbsp hummus

4 thin slices cooked turkey

½ tbsp toasted sunflower seeds

1 whole wheat pita

salt and pepper

Method

1 Preheat the broiler to high.

2 Put the spinach leaves, bell pepper, carrot, and hummus into a large bowl and stir together, so all the salad ingredients are coated with the hummus. Stir in the turkey and sunflower seeds and season to taste with salt and pepper.

3 Put the pita under the preheated broiler for about 1 minute on each side to warm through, but do not brown. Cut it in half to make 2 "pockets."

4 Divide the filling between the pita pockets. Wrap in foil for a brown bag lunch.

creamy tomato soup

Serves 4–6

Ingredients

1 lb 2 oz/500 g ripe tomatoes

1 tbsp butter

½ red onion, finely chopped

1 leek, chopped

1 garlic clove, crushed

1 carrot, peeled and grated

1 potato, peeled and grated

1¼ cups vegetable stock

1 tbsp tomato paste

⅔ cup milk

salt and pepper

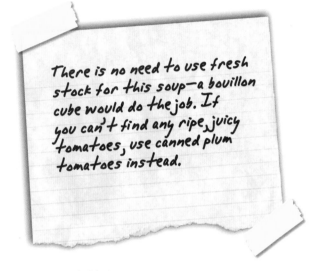

There is no need to use fresh stock for this soup—a bouillon cube would do the job. If you can't find any ripe, juicy tomatoes, use canned plum tomatoes instead.

Method

1 Make a cross in the top of each tomato, then place in a bowl of boiling water for 5–10 minutes, or until the skins have split. Remove with a slotted spoon and transfer to a bowl of ice water. Drain the tomatoes well and peel off the skins. Cut into wedges, then remove and discard the seeds. Coarsely chop the tomato flesh and set aside.

2 Melt the butter in a large pan over low heat and cook the onion, leek, and garlic for 10 minutes, or until very soft but not browned.

3 Add the carrot and potato and cook for 5 minutes. Add the stock and bring up to simmering point.

4 Add the tomatoes and tomato paste and season to taste with salt and pepper. Let simmer for 15 minutes until the vegetables are very soft. Add the milk and warm through, then liquidize the soup in the pan using a handheld stick blender. You can pass the soup through a strainer at this stage, if you like.

5 Ladle the soup into serving bowls or transfer to a thermos for a brown bag lunch.

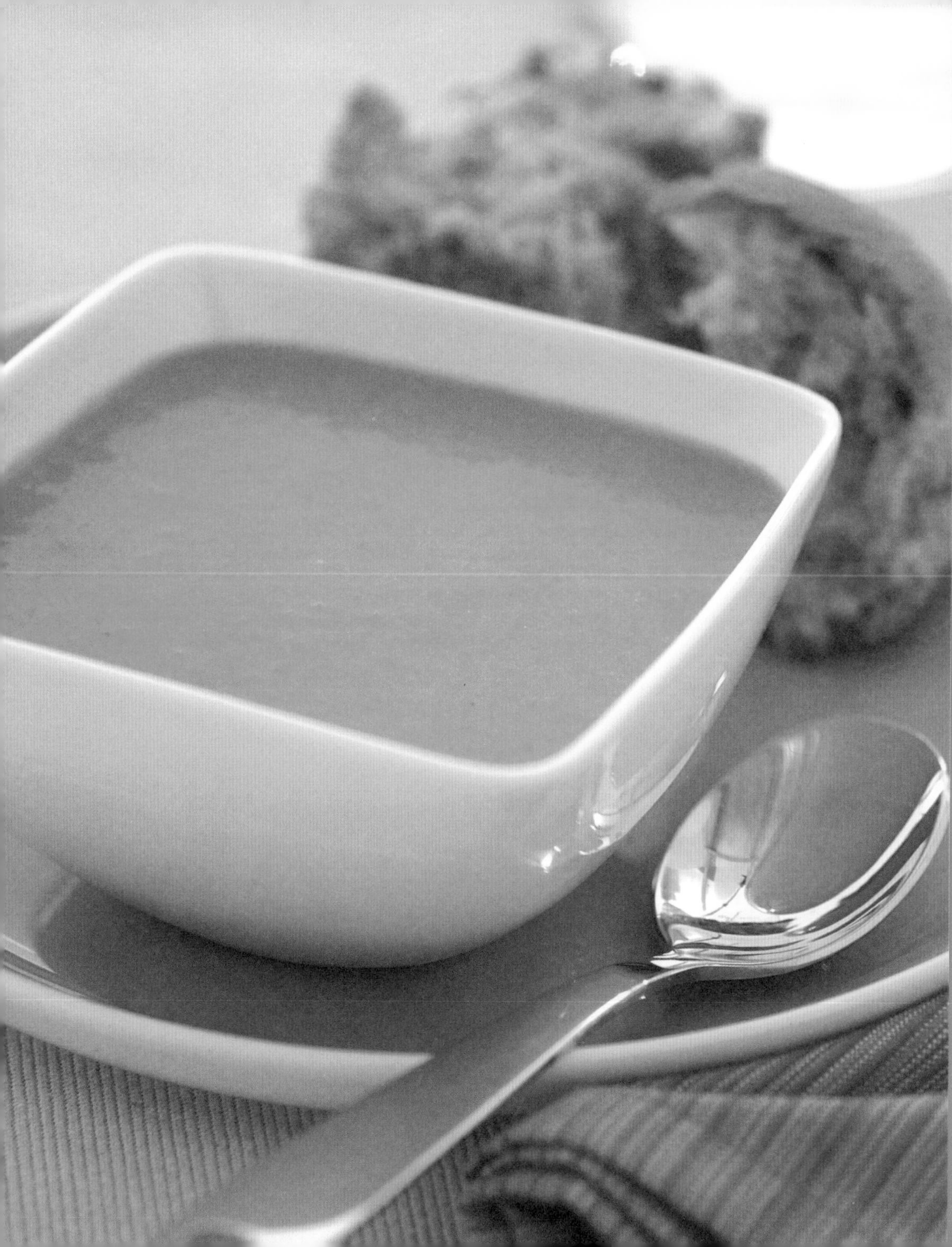

leek & potato soup

Serves 4–6

Ingredients

4 tbsp butter

1 onion, chopped

3 leeks, sliced

8 oz/225 g potatoes, peeled and cut into
¾-inch/2-cm cubes

3½ cups vegetable stock

⅔ cup light cream (optional)

salt and pepper

fresh flat-leaf parsley sprigs, to garnish (optional)

Method

1 Melt the butter in a large saucepan over medium heat, add the onion, leeks, and potatoes, and sauté gently for 2–3 minutes, until softened but not browned. Pour in the stock, bring to a boil, then reduce the heat and simmer, covered, for 15 minutes.

2 Remove from the heat and liquidize the soup in the pan using a handheld stick blender.

3 Reheat the soup, season to taste with salt and pepper, and transfer to serving bowls. Swirl with the cream, if using, and garnish with parsley sprigs, if using. Alternatively, transfer to a thermos for a brown bag lunch.

chicken noodle soup

Serves 4

Ingredients

2 skinless, boneless chicken breasts

5 cups water or chicken stock

3 carrots, peeled and cut into ¼-inch/5-mm slices

3 oz/85 g vermicelli (or other fine noodles)

salt and pepper

fresh tarragon leaves, to garnish (optional)

Method

1 Place the chicken breasts in a large saucepan, add the water, and bring to a simmer. Cook for 25–30 minutes. Skim any foam from the surface, if necessary. Remove the chicken from the liquid and keep warm.

2 Continue to simmer, add the carrots and vermicelli, and cook for 4–5 minutes.

3 Thinly slice or shred the chicken breasts and place in serving dishes.

4 Season the soup to taste with salt and pepper, pour over the chicken, and garnish with tarragon leaves, if using. Alternatively, stir the chicken and tarragon, if using, into the soup and transfer to a thermos for a brown bag lunch.

Store any leftover soup in an airtight container in the fridge, or freeze for another day.

spicy red lentil soup

Serves 4

Ingredients

10½ oz/300 g red lentils, rinsed

8 cups vegetable stock or water

2 fresh green chiles, split

1 tsp turmeric

2 tbsp sunflower oil

1½ onions, thinly sliced

2 large garlic cloves, crushed

2 tsp curry paste, mild, medium, or hot, to taste

salt and pepper

4 tbsp Greek-style yogurt and chopped fresh cilantro leaves, to garnish (optional)

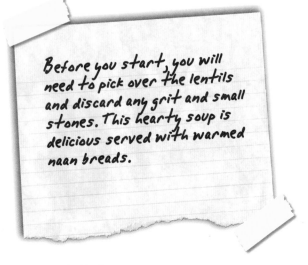

Before you start, you will need to pick over the lentils and discard any grit and small stones. This hearty soup is delicious served with warmed naan breads.

Method

1 Put the lentils and stock into a large pan with a tight-fitting lid. Place over high heat and slowly bring to a boil, skimming the surface as necessary. Add the chiles and turmeric, reduce the heat to very low, cover the pan, and let the lentils simmer for 25–30 minutes, until they are very soft and mushy.

2 Meanwhile, heat the oil in a separate large pan over medium heat. Add the onions and garlic and fry for 5–7 minutes, until the onions are tender but not brown. Add the curry paste and cook, stirring, for about a minute.

3 Liquidize the soup in the pan using a handheld stick blender. Add a little water to thin the soup, if wished, then slowly bring to a boil, reduce the heat, and simmer for 2 minutes. Season to taste with salt and pepper.

4 Ladle the soup into serving dishes, then drizzle over a little Greek yogurt and scatter with cilantro, if using. Alternatively, transfer to a thermos for a brown bag lunch.

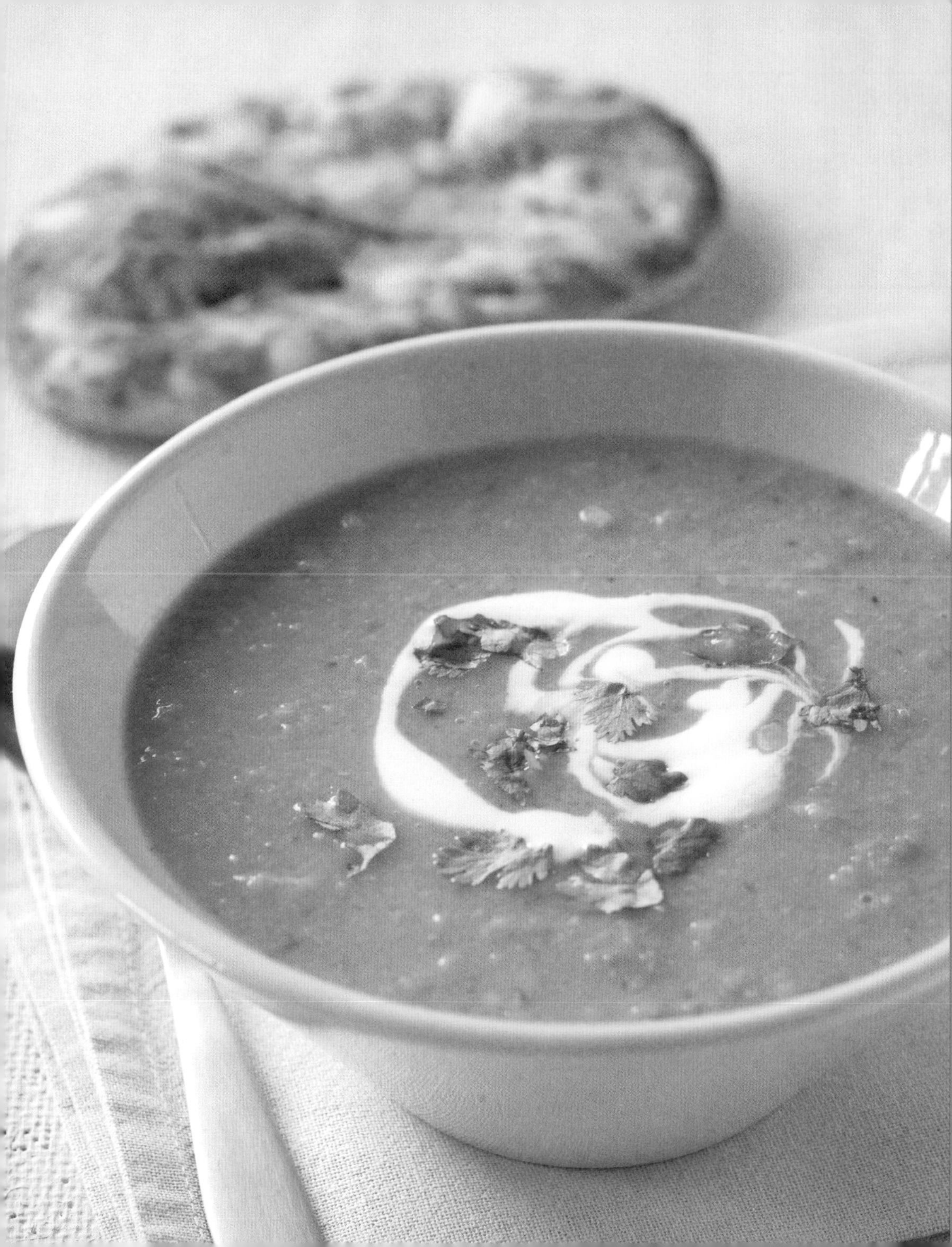

spanish omelet

Serves 2

Ingredients

7 oz/200 g new potatoes

1 tbsp olive oil

1 onion, thinly sliced

1 red bell pepper, seeded and thinly sliced

2 tomatoes, peeled, seeded, and chopped

6 large eggs

1 tbsp milk

2 tbsp finely grated Parmesan cheese

salt and pepper

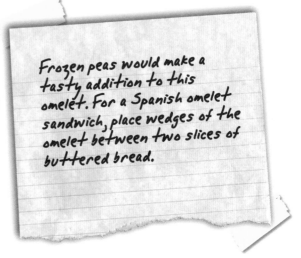

Frozen peas would make a tasty addition to this omelet. For a Spanish omelet sandwich, place wedges of the omelet between two slices of buttered bread.

Method

1 Cook the potatoes in a pan of boiling water for 8–12 minutes, until tender. Drain and let cool, then slice.

2 Heat the oil in a 7–8-inch/18–20-cm skillet with a heatproof handle and cook the onion and bell pepper until soft. Add the tomatoes and cook for an additional minute.

3 Add the potatoes to the skillet and spread out evenly.

4 Beat the eggs, milk, cheese, and salt and pepper to taste in a bowl and pour over the potato mixture. Cook for 4–5 minutes, until the eggs are set underneath.

5 Meanwhile, preheat the broiler to high. Place the skillet under the broiler and cook the omelet for an additional 3–4 minutes, until the eggs are set.

6 Serve immediately or let cool, then cut into wedges and wrap in foil for a brown bag lunch.

cheesy corn fritters

Serves 2

Ingredients

1 egg

scant 1 cup milk

¾ cup all-purpose flour

½ tsp baking powder

3 oz/85 g canned corn kernels, drained

4 tbsp grated cheddar cheese

1 tsp snipped fresh chives

2 tsp sunflower oil

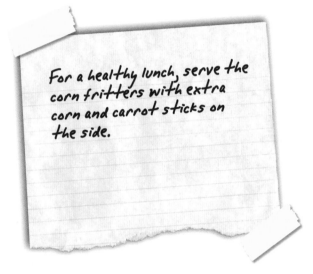

For a healthy lunch, serve the corn fritters with extra corn and carrot sticks on the side.

Method

1 Put the egg and milk into a small bowl and beat with a fork. Add the flour and baking powder and beat until smooth. Stir in the corn, cheese, and chives.

2 Heat the oil in a skillet and drop either teaspoonfuls or tablespoonfuls of the batter into it. Cook for 1–2 minutes on each side, until the fritters are puffed up and golden.

3 Drain on paper towels and serve immediately or let cool, then wrap in foil for a brown bag lunch.

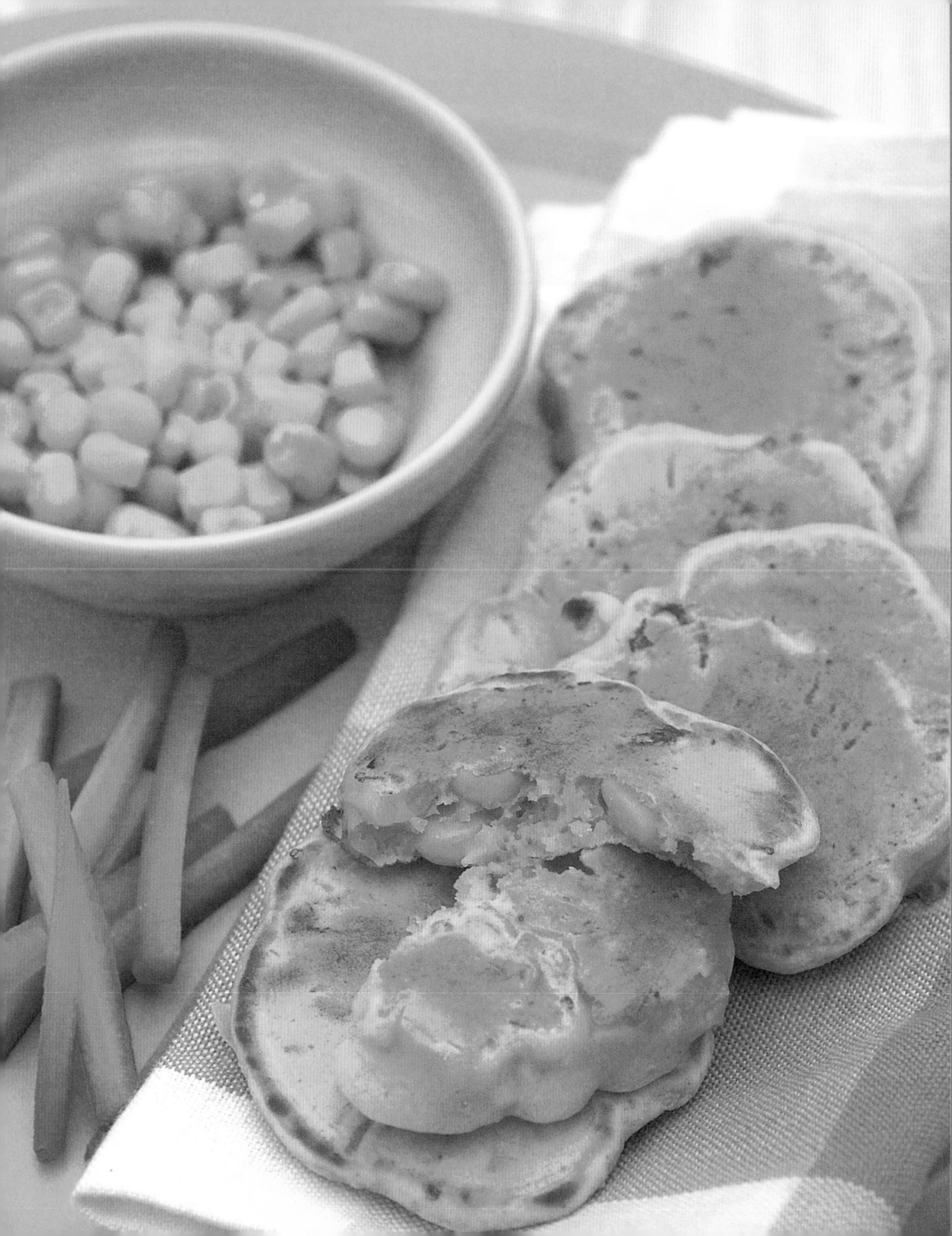

bread, onion & tomato salad

Serves 2

Ingredients

2–3 bread rolls, depending on size

3 tbsp white wine vinegar

5 tbsp extra virgin olive oil

6 slices salami

1 tomato

1 large onion

1 scallion

salt and pepper

Method

1 Break the bread rolls into pieces and place in a bowl. Pour over the vinegar and oil and let stand for 10 minutes, stirring frequently.

2 Chop up the salami and tomato.

3 Peel the onion, halve it, and cut into slices lengthwise.

4 Add all of the chopped ingredients to the bread mixture. Season to taste with salt and pepper.

5 Mix together carefully. Finely chop the scallion and scatter over the salad before serving. Transfer to an airtight container for a brown bag lunch.

roasted vegetable salad

Serves 4

Ingredients

1 onion

1 eggplant

1 red bell pepper, seeded

1 orange bell pepper, seeded

1 large zucchini

2–4 garlic cloves

2–4 tbsp olive oil

1 tbsp balsamic vinegar

2 tbsp extra virgin olive oil

1 tbsp shredded fresh basil

salt and pepper

Parmesan cheese shavings, to serve (optional)

Method

1 Preheat the oven to 400°F/200°C. Cut all the vegetables into even-size wedges, put into a roasting pan, and scatter over the garlic. Pour over 2 tablespoons of the olive oil and toss the vegetables until well coated with the oil. Season to taste with salt and pepper. Roast in the preheated oven for 40 minutes, or until tender, adding more olive oil if needed.

2 Meanwhile, put the vinegar, extra virgin olive oil, and salt and pepper to taste into a screw-top jar and shake until blended.

3 When the vegetables are cooked, remove from the oven, arrange on a serving dish, and pour over the dressing. Sprinkle with the basil and serve with Parmesan cheese shavings, if using. Alternatively, let cool, then transfer to an airtight container for a brown bag lunch.

Salads are great for a brown bag lunch—store in a mini cool box to keep them fresh until lunchtime.

pasta salad

Serves 2

Ingredients

3½ oz/100 g dried pasta spirals

2 tbsp olive oil, plus extra if needed

1 tbsp mayonnaise

1 tbsp plain yogurt

2 tbsp pesto

7 oz/200 g canned tuna, drained
   and flaked

7 oz/200 g canned corn kernels, drained

2 tomatoes, peeled, seeded, and chopped

½ green bell pepper, seeded and chopped

½ avocado, pitted, peeled, and chopped

salt and pepper

Pasta salads are incredibly versatile—just add any salad ingredients you have to hand. Vegetarians could use drained canned beans in place of the tuna.

Method

1 Bring a large pan of lightly salted water to a boil. Add the pasta, return to a boil, and cook for 8–10 minutes, until tender but still firm to the bite. Drain, return to the pan, and add the oil. Toss well to coat, then cover and let cool.

2 Whisk the mayonnaise, yogurt, and pesto together in a pitcher, adding a little oil if needed to achieve the desired consistency. Add a pinch of salt and season to taste with pepper.

3 Mix the cooled pasta with the tuna, corn, tomatoes, bell pepper, and avocado, add the dressing, and toss well to coat. Serve immediately or transfer to an airtight container for a brown bag lunch.

STUDENT TASTE TEAM

Name: Dan Toy

Studying: Writing for Publication, Performance and Media

At: Pratt Institute, NY USA

Comments about dish: This recipe necessitated inexpensive ingredients and was easy to make

Marks:
9/10

rice salad

Serves 2

Ingredients

1 leek

1 red bell pepper

5¾ oz/160 g canned corn kernels

4½ cups cooked long-grain rice

5 basil leaves

3 tbsp white wine vinegar

2 tbsp olive oil

salt and pepper

Method

1 Slice the leek into thin rings.

2 Wash the bell pepper, seed, and chop into ½-inch/1-cm cubes. Drain the corn.

3 Put the bell pepper, leek, and corn into a large bowl with the rice. Slice the basil leaves into strips and put them into the bowl.

4 Mix together the vinegar and oil in a small bowl, then season to taste with salt and pepper and pour over the rice salad.

5 Mix everything together well. Serve immediately or transfer to an airtight container for a brown bag lunch.

tabbouleh

Serves 4

Ingredients

scant 1 cup bulgur wheat

3 tbsp extra virgin olive oil

4 tbsp lemon juice

4 scallions

1 green bell pepper, seeded and sliced

4 tomatoes, chopped

2 tbsp chopped fresh parsley

2 tbsp chopped fresh mint

8 black olives, pitted

salt and pepper

Method

1 Place the bulgur wheat in a large bowl and add enough cold water to cover. Let it stand for 30 minutes, or until it has doubled in size. Drain well and press out as much liquid as possible. Spread out the wheat on paper towels to dry.

2 Place the wheat in a serving bowl. Mix the oil and lemon juice together in a pitcher and season to taste with salt and pepper. Pour the lemon mixture over the wheat and let marinate for 1 hour.

3 Using a sharp knife, finely chop the scallions, then add to the salad with the bell pepper, tomatoes, parsley, and mint and toss lightly to mix. Top the salad with the olives. Serve immediately or transfer to an airtight container for a brown bag lunch.

Save money by keeping pots of fresh herbs on your windowsill to use each time you cook.

barbecued chicken

Serves 4

Ingredients

4 chicken drumsticks, skinned

finely chopped scallions,
   to garnish (optional)

Barbecue sauce

1 shallot, finely chopped

1 garlic clove, crushed

1 tbsp tomato paste, blended with
   ⅔ cup water

2 tbsp red wine vinegar

1 tbsp prepared mustard

1 tbsp Worcestershire sauce

These piquant chicken drumsticks are equally delicious served hot or cold. Chicken drumsticks are much cheaper than chicken breasts, although you could use either for this recipe.

Method

1 To make the sauce, place the shallot, garlic, tomato paste mixture, vinegar, mustard, and Worcestershire sauce in a screw-top jar, cover with the lid, and shake vigorously until well blended.

2 Rinse the chicken drumsticks and pat dry with paper towels. Place the drumsticks in a large, ovenproof dish, pour over the sauce, and let stand for at least 2 hours, occasionally spooning the sauce over the chicken.

3 Preheat the oven to 375°F/190°C. Cook the chicken drumsticks in the preheated oven for 20–25 minutes, or until the juices run clear when a skewer is inserted into the thickest part of the meat. Spoon the sauce over the chicken or turn the chicken over during cooking.

4 Serve immediately, garnished with scallions, if using. Alternatively, let cool, then transfer to an airtight container for a brown bag lunch.

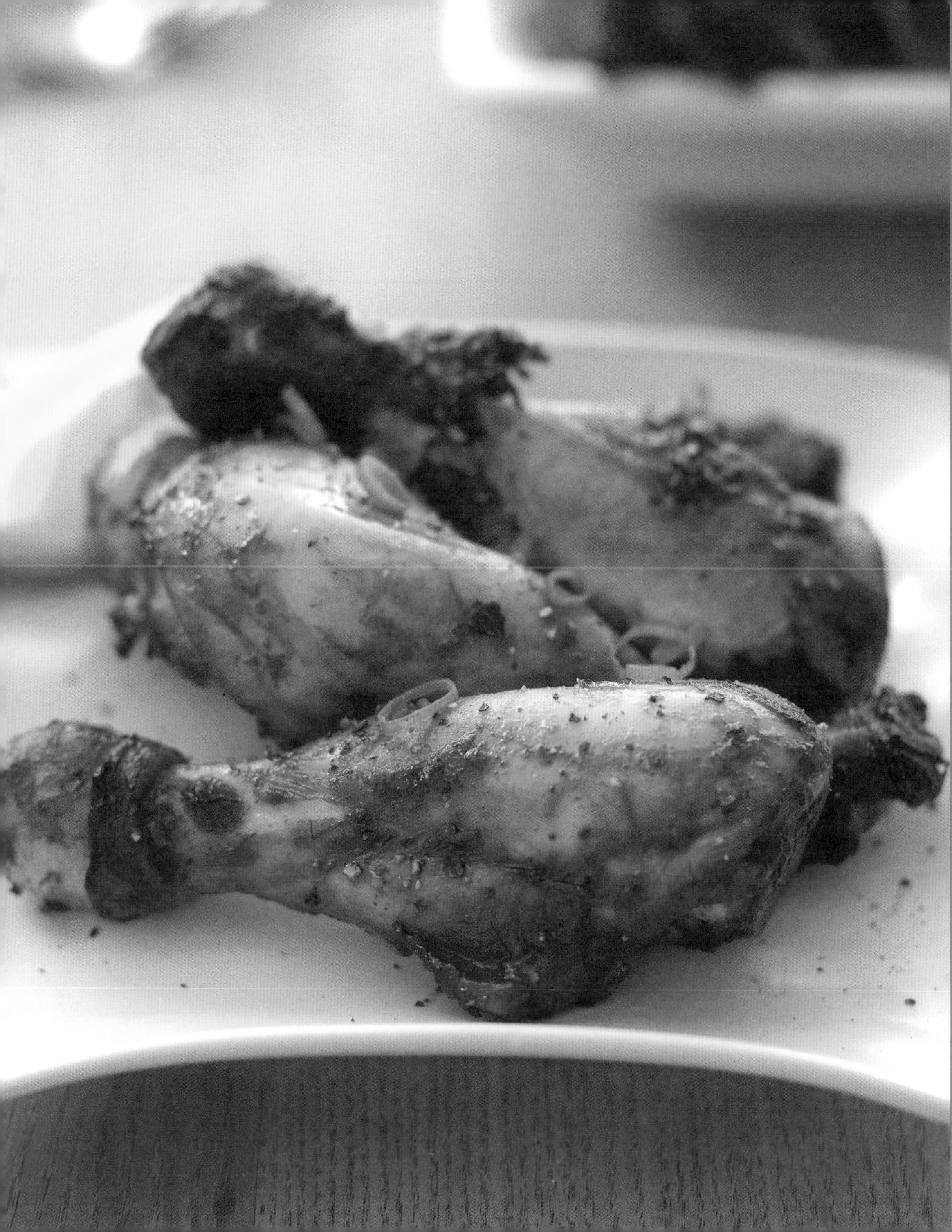

mini ham & cheese pastries

Makes 6

Ingredients

butter, for greasing

7 oz/200 g prepared puff pastry, thawed if frozen

all-purpose flour, for dusting

3 eggs, beaten

½ cup milk

¾ cup grated sharp cheddar cheese

1 slice cooked ham, chopped

1 tomato, sliced

salt and pepper

Method

1 Preheat the oven to 400°F/200°C. Grease a 6-cup muffin pan.

2 Roll the pastry out on a lightly floured work surface until it is very thin. Cut out 6 circles to fit the cups in the muffin pan, making sure that the pastry extends just above the rim.

3 Whisk the eggs and milk together in a bowl and season to taste with salt and pepper. Divide the cheese among the pastry shells. Sprinkle over the ham, then pour the egg mixture over the top. Top each with a tomato slice.

4 Bake in the preheated oven for 20–25 minutes, or until risen and golden. Let cool slightly before removing from the pan.

cheese sticks

Serves 4–6

Ingredients

butter, for greasing

13 oz/375 g prepared puff pastry, thawed if frozen

all-purpose flour, for dusting

¾ cup grated Gruyère cheese

½ tsp paprika

1 egg, beaten

Method

1 Preheat the oven to 400°F/200°C. Grease a large baking sheet.

2 Roll the pastry out on a lightly floured work surface until it is thin. Mix together the Gruyère cheese and paprika and sprinkle over the sheet of pastry. Fold the pastry in half and roll out a little to seal the edges.

3 Cut the pastry into long ½ inch/1 cm wide strips, then cut each strip in half and gently twist. Place on the prepared baking sheet. Brush with the beaten egg and bake in the preheated oven for 10–12 minutes, or until crisp and golden. Let cool on a wire rack.

Making fresh puff pastry is incredibly fiddly and time-consuming so it's really worth splashing out on prepared pastry.

banana loaf

Serves 8

Ingredients

butter, for greasing

scant 1 cup white self-rising flour

scant ¾ cup light brown self-rising flour

generous ¾ cup raw brown sugar

pinch of salt

½ tsp ground cinnamon

½ tsp ground nutmeg

2 large ripe bananas, peeled

¾ cup orange juice

2 eggs, beaten

4 tbsp sunflower oil

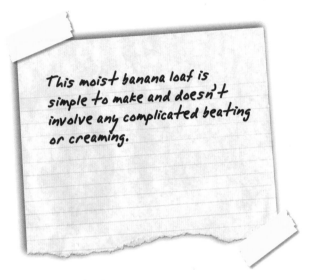

This moist banana loaf is simple to make and doesn't involve any complicated beating or creaming.

Method

1 Preheat the oven to 350°F/180°C. Lightly grease a 9 x 5 x 3-inch/23 x 13 x 8-cm loaf pan and line with parchment paper.

2 Sift the flours, sugar, salt, and the spices into a large bowl. In a separate bowl, mash the bananas with the orange juice, then stir in the eggs and oil. Pour into the dry ingredients and mix well.

3 Spoon into the prepared loaf pan and bake in the preheated oven for 1 hour, then test to see if the loaf is cooked by inserting a skewer into the center. If it comes out clean, the loaf is done. If not, bake for an additional 10 minutes and test again.

4 Remove from the oven and let cool in the pan. Turn out the loaf, slice, and serve.

peanut butter cookies

Makes 26

Ingredients

½ cup softened butter,
plus extra for greasing

scant ½ cup crunchy peanut butter

generous ½ cup superfine sugar

generous ½ cup light brown sugar

1 egg, beaten

½ tsp vanilla extract

⅔ cup all-purpose flour

½ tsp baking soda

½ tsp baking powder

pinch of salt

1½ cups rolled oats

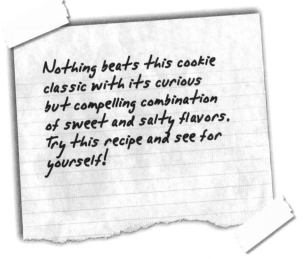

Nothing beats this cookie classic with its curious but compelling combination of sweet and salty flavors. Try this recipe and see for yourself!

Method

1 Preheat the oven to 350°F/180°C. Grease a large baking sheet.

2 Place the butter and peanut butter in a bowl and beat together. Beat in the superfine sugar and brown sugar, then gradually beat in the egg and vanilla extract.

3 Sift the flour, baking soda, baking powder, and salt into the bowl and stir in the oats.

4 Place spoonfuls of the cookie dough onto the prepared baking sheet, spaced well apart to allow for spreading. Flatten slightly with a fork.

5 Bake in the preheated oven for 12 minutes, or until lightly browned. Let cool on the baking sheet for 2 minutes, then transfer to a wire rack to cool completely.

STUDENT TASTE TEAM

Name: Charlotte Hawken
Studying: Sociology
At: Bristol University, UK
Comments about dish: The recipe was really easy—I would definitely recommend it

Marks:
8/10

orange oat bars

Makes 18

Ingredients

¾ cup unsalted butter, plus extra for greasing

scant ¾ cup dark corn syrup

⅓ cup raw brown sugar

2 cups rolled oats

⅔ cup whole wheat flour

½ cup raisins or golden raisins

finely grated rind of 1 large orange

Method

1 Preheat the oven to 375°F/180°C. Grease a 10 x 8-inch/25 x 20-cm baking pan and line with parchment paper.

2 Put the butter, corn syrup, and sugar into a pan over high heat and stir until the butter and syrup have melted and the sugar has dissolved, then bring to a boil without stirring.

3 Put the oats, flour, raisins, and orange rind into a large mixing bowl. Pour in the butter mixture and stir all the ingredients together. Tip into the prepared pan and use the back of a wooden spoon to spread it evenly over the bottom of the pan and into the corners.

4 Bake in the preheated oven for 25–30 minutes, until the mixture has set. Let cool completely in the pan. When cool, cut into thick bars.

no-bake chocolate cake

Serves 6–8

Ingredients

8 oz/225 g semisweet chocolate, broken into pieces

1 cup unsalted butter, plus extra for greasing

3 tbsp black coffee

¼ cup light brown sugar

a few drops of vanilla extract

8 oz/225 g graham crackers, crushed

½ cup raisins

¾ cup walnuts, chopped

Method

1 Grease a 8 x 4 x 2-inch/20 x 10 x 5-cm loaf pan and line with parchment paper. Melt the chocolate, butter, coffee, sugar, and vanilla extract in a pan over low heat.

2 Add the crushed crackers, raisins, and walnuts and stir well.

3 Spoon the mixture into the prepared loaf pan.

4 Let set for 1–2 hours in the refrigerator, then turn out and cut into thin slices.

These tasty treats are perfect mid-morning or afternoon snacks. Store in an airtight container for up to 1 week—if they last that long!

simple suppers

There's nothing worse than getting home in the evening and not having a clue what to cook. You're hungry and your brain is so frazzled that just thinking about dinner makes your head hurt! That's where this chapter comes in with its selection of supper solutions. The recipes are so straightforward that even novice cooks can't fail to be impressed. What's more, many are super speedy and can be on your plate within half an hour.

baked chile cheese sandwiches

Serves 2–4

Ingredients

3½ cups grated cheese, such as cheddar

8 tbsp softened butter

4 fresh green chiles, seeded and chopped

½ tsp ground cumin

8 thick slices bread, each buttered on one side

Method

1 Preheat the oven to 375°F/190°C. Mix the cheese and butter together in a bowl until creamy, then add the chiles and cumin.

2 Place 4 slices of the bread, buttered-side down, on a baking sheet, then spread with the cheese mixture. Top with the remaining slices of bread, buttered-side up, and press down.

3 Bake in the preheated oven for 8–10 minutes, until crisp and lightly browned. Serve immediately.

mini muffin pizzas

Serves 3

Ingredients

3 English muffins, split

2 tbsp tomato paste

2 tbsp pesto

1 tbsp olive oil

½ red onion, thinly sliced

3 mushrooms, sliced

½ zucchini, thinly sliced

2–3 slices cooked ham or 6 slices salami

scant 1 cup grated cheddar cheese or 6 slices mozzarella cheese

Method

1 Preheat the broiler to high. Toast the English muffins under the preheated broiler until golden, then let cool.

2 Mix the tomato paste and pesto together in a small bowl and spread equally over the muffin halves.

3 Heat the oil in a nonstick skillet and then cook the onion, mushrooms, and zucchini until soft and beginning to brown.

4 Divide the vegetables among the muffin halves, top with the ham, then the cheese.

5 Cook under the broiler for 3–4 minutes, until the cheese is melted and browned. Serve hot or cold.

The chile cheese sandwiches can be cooked in a toaster oven, if you have one.

italian steak sandwiches

Serves 4

Ingredients

1 tbsp olive oil, plus extra for brushing

1 small onion, finely chopped

1 garlic clove, finely chopped

1 small red bell pepper, seeded and
finely chopped

1⅓ cups chopped mushrooms

scant 1 cup ground beef

½ cup red wine

2 tbsp tomato paste

4 bread rolls

4 slices mozzarella cheese

2 tbsp torn fresh basil leaves

salt and pepper

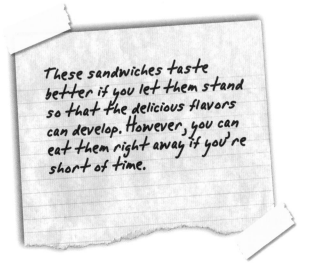

These sandwiches taste better if you let them stand so that the delicious flavors can develop. However, you can eat them right away if you're short of time.

Method

1 Heat the oil in a large pan over medium heat. Add the onion, garlic, bell pepper, and mushrooms, and cook, stirring occasionally, for 5–10 minutes, until softened and beginning to brown.

2 Add the beef and cook, stirring frequently and breaking up any lumps with a wooden spoon, for 5 minutes, or until browned on all sides. Add the wine, tomato paste, and salt and pepper to taste and let simmer for 10 minutes, stirring occasionally. Remove from the heat.

3 Preheat the broiler to medium–high. Split the bread rolls in half and brush both halves with oil. Toast lightly under the preheated broiler. Put the bottom halves onto a piece of foil and spoon an equal quantity of the sauce on top of each.

4 Divide the cheese among the roll bottoms and arrange on top of the sauce. Add the basil leaves and cover with the tops of the rolls. Press down gently and wrap in the foil. Let the sandwiches stand for at least 1 hour before serving.

mushroom fajitas

Serves 4–8

Ingredients

1 lb 2 oz/500 g portobello mushrooms

2 tbsp corn oil

1 onion, sliced

1 red bell pepper, seeded and sliced

1 green bell pepper, seeded and sliced

1 garlic clove, crushed

¼–½ tsp cayenne pepper

juice and grated rind of 2 limes

2 tsp sugar

1 tsp dried oregano

8 flour tortillas

salt and pepper

lime wedges, to garnish

Method

1 Cut the mushrooms into strips. Heat the oil in a large, heavy-bottom skillet. Add the mushrooms, onion, bell peppers, and garlic and stir-fry for 8–10 minutes, until the vegetables are cooked.

2 Add the cayenne pepper, lime juice and rind, sugar, and oregano. Season to taste with salt and pepper and cook for an additional 2 minutes.

3 Meanwhile, heat the tortillas according to the package directions. Divide the mushroom mixture among the warmed tortillas and roll up. Serve immediately, garnished with lime wedges.

chorizo & cheese quesadillas

Serves 4

Ingredients

1 cup grated mozzarella cheese

1 cup grated cheddar cheese

8 oz/225 g cooked chorizo sausage (outer casing removed), diced

4 scallions, finely chopped

2 fresh green chiles, seeded and finely chopped

8 flour tortillas

corn oil, for brushing

salt and pepper

Method

1 Place the cheeses, chorizo, scallions, chiles, and salt and pepper to taste in a bowl and mix together.

2 Divide the mixture among 4 of the tortillas, then top with the remaining tortillas.

3 Brush a large, heavy-bottom skillet with oil and heat over medium heat. Add a quesadilla and cook, pressing it down with a spatula, for 4–5 minutes, until the underside is crisp and lightly browned. Turn over and cook the other side until the cheese has melted. Remove from the skillet and keep warm. Cook the remaining quesadillas.

4 Cut each quesadilla into quarters, arrange on a serving plate, and serve immediately.

These Mexican favorites are great for chilled-out nights in with a bunch of friends and a DVD. Serve with sour cream, salsa, and guacamole.

chinese rice with omelet strips

Serves 2

Ingredients

2 tsp vegetable oil

a few drops of sesame oil

1 small garlic clove, finely chopped

pinch of Chinese five spice

1 carrot, peeled and diced

2 baby corn, halved and thinly sliced

2 tbsp water

small handful of baby spinach, tough stems removed, finely sliced

1¼ cups cold cooked brown or white rice

dash of soy sauce

1 tsp sesame seeds (optional)

small pat of butter

1 egg, beaten

This recipe turns leftover rice into a tasty and filling meal. Make sure to store cooked rice in the refrigerator and use within 1-2 days.

STUDENT TASTE TEAM

Name: Laura Dickson

Studying: Art History and Archaeology

At: Universität Bonn, Germany

Comments about dish: I would cook this again

Marks: 8/10

Method

1 Heat the vegetable oil and sesame oil in a wok or heavy-bottom skillet. Add the garlic, five spice, carrot, and baby corn and stir-fry for 5 minutes, stirring and tossing continuously to prevent the spices and vegetables from burning and sticking.

2 Add the water and stir-fry for 2 minutes, then mix in the spinach and cook, stirring frequently, for an additional 2 minutes, or until the vegetables are tender.

3 Add the rice and soy sauce to the wok and heat through thoroughly. Mix in the sesame seeds, if using.

4 Meanwhile, melt the butter in a small, heavy-bottom skillet and add the egg. Swirl the egg until it covers the bottom of the skillet. Cook until the egg has set and is cooked through, then turn out onto a plate. Cut the omelet into strips or pieces.

5 Place the rice in a bowl and arrange the omelet on top.

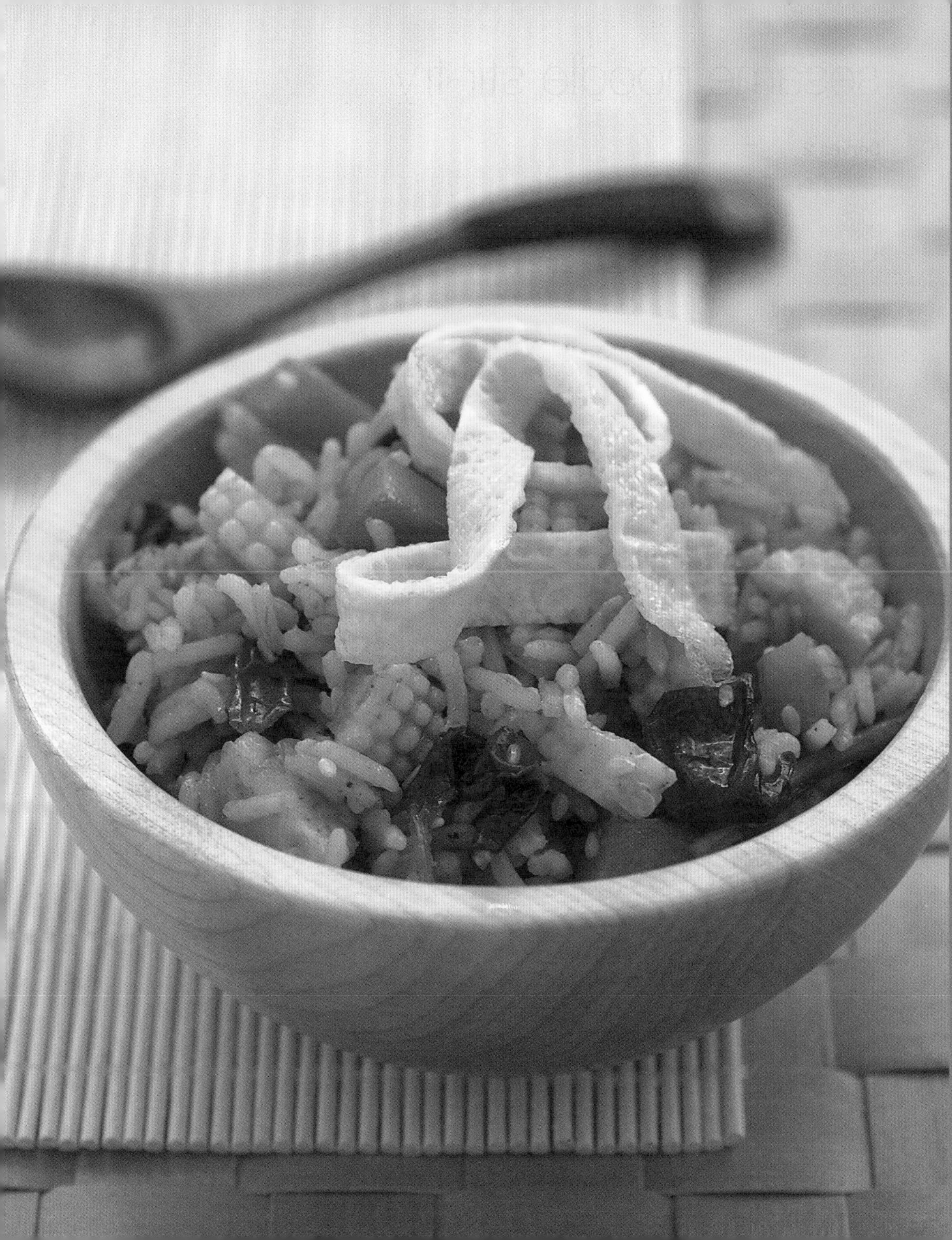

sesame noodle stir-fry

Serves 2

Ingredients

1 tsp red wine vinegar

1 tbsp soy sauce

1 tbsp ketchup

2 tbsp orange juice

1 tsp honey

1 tsp cornstarch

1 tbsp vegetable oil

3½ oz/100 g skinless, boneless chicken breast, cut into strips

2 scallions, finely sliced

2 oz/55 g baby corn, halved lengthwise

1 carrot, peeled and cut into thin sticks

½ red bell pepper, seeded and chopped

½ zucchini, chopped

1¾ oz/50 g dried fine egg noodles

2 tsp sesame seeds

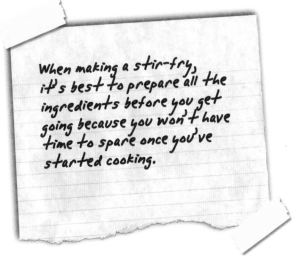

When making a stir-fry, it's best to prepare all the ingredients before you get going because you won't have time to spare once you've started cooking.

Method

1 Mix the vinegar, soy sauce, ketchup, orange juice, and honey together in a pitcher, add the cornstarch, and stir until well combined.

2 Heat the oil in a nonstick skillet and stir-fry the chicken for 3–4 minutes. Add the vegetables and stir-fry for 4–5 minutes.

3 Add the cornstarch mixture and bring to a boil, stirring constantly, then reduce the heat and let simmer for 1 minute, until thickened.

4 Meanwhile, cook the noodles according to the package directions, drain, and add to the skillet along with the sesame seeds. Mix well. Serve immediately.

spaghetti olio e aglio

Serves 4

Ingredients

1 lb/450 g dried spaghetti

½ cup extra virgin olive oil

3 garlic cloves, finely chopped

3 tbsp chopped fresh flat-leaf parsley

salt and pepper

Method

1 Bring a large pan of lightly salted water to a boil. Add the pasta, return to a boil, and cook for 8–10 minutes, or until tender but still firm to the bite.

2 Meanwhile, heat the oil in a skillet. Add the garlic and a pinch of salt and cook over low heat, stirring constantly, for 3–4 minutes, or until golden. Do not let the garlic brown or it will taste bitter. Remove the skillet from the heat.

3 Drain the pasta and transfer to a serving dish. Pour in the garlic-flavored olive oil, then add the parsley and season to taste with salt and pepper. Toss well and serve immediately.

spaghetti with tomatoes & basil

Serves 4

Ingredients

5 tbsp extra virgin olive oil

1 onion, finely chopped

1 lb 12 oz/800 g canned chopped tomatoes

4 garlic cloves, cut into quarters

1 lb/450 g dried spaghetti

large handful fresh basil leaves, shredded

salt and pepper

Parmesan cheese shavings, to serve

Method

1 Heat the oil in a large pan over medium heat. Add the onion and cook gently for 5 minutes, until soft. Add the tomatoes and garlic. Bring to a boil, then simmer over low–medium heat for 25–30 minutes, or until the oil separates from the tomato. Season to taste with salt and pepper.

2 Bring a large pan of lightly salted water to a boil. Add the pasta, return to a boil, and cook for 8–10 minutes, or until tender but still firm to the bite. Drain and transfer to a serving dish.

3 Pour the sauce over the pasta. Add the basil and toss well to mix. Serve with Parmesan shavings.

88

mushroom & spinach pasta

Serves 4

Ingredients

10½ oz/300 g dried pasta

2 tbsp olive oil

2¾ cups sliced mushrooms

1 tsp dried oregano

scant 1¼ cups vegetable stock

1 tbsp lemon juice

6 tbsp cream cheese

1 cup frozen spinach leaves

salt and pepper

Method

1 Bring a large pan of lightly salted water to a boil. Add the pasta, return to a boil, and cook for 8–10 minutes, until tender but still firm to the bite. Drain, reserving ¾ cup of the cooking liquid.

2 Meanwhile, heat the oil in a large skillet, add the mushrooms, and cook, stirring frequently, for 8 minutes. Stir in the oregano, stock, and lemon juice and cook for 10–12 minutes, or until reduced by half.

3 Stir in the cream cheese and spinach and cook over low–medium heat for 3–5 minutes. Add the reserved cooking liquid, then the cooked pasta. Stir well, season to taste with salt and pepper, and heat through before serving.

spaghetti alla carbonara

Serves 4

Ingredients

1 lb/450 g dried spaghetti

1 tbsp olive oil

8 oz/225 g bacon, chopped

4 eggs

5 tbsp light cream

2 tbsp grated Parmesan cheese

salt and pepper

Method

1 Bring a large pan of lightly salted water to a boil. Add the pasta, return to a boil, and cook for 8–10 minutes, or until tender but still firm to the bite.

2 Meanwhile, heat the oil in a skillet. Add the bacon and cook over medium heat, stirring frequently, for 8–10 minutes.

3 Beat the eggs with the cream in a small bowl and season to taste with salt and pepper. Drain the pasta and return it to the pan. Turn in the contents of the skillet, then add the egg mixture and half the Parmesan cheese. Stir well, then transfer to a serving dish. Serve immediately, sprinkled with the remaining cheese.

tuna-noodle casserole

Serves 4–6

Ingredients

7 oz/200 g dried egg ribbon pasta, such as tagliatelle

2 tbsp butter

1 cup fine fresh breadcrumbs

14 oz/400 g condensed canned cream of mushroom soup

½ cup milk

2 celery stalks, chopped

1 red and 1 green bell pepper, seeded and chopped

1¼ cups grated sharp cheddar cheese

2 tbsp chopped fresh parsley

7 oz/200 g canned tuna in oil, drained and flaked

salt and pepper

This recipe can easily be adapted to suit your tastes. For example, vegetarians can omit the tuna and add a couple of handfuls of chopped mushrooms.

Method

1 Preheat the oven to 400°F/200°C. Bring a large pan of lightly salted water to a boil. Add the pasta, return to a boil, and cook for 2 minutes fewer than specified on the package directions.

2 Meanwhile, melt the butter in a separate small pan over medium heat. Stir in the breadcrumbs, then remove from the heat and set aside.

3 Drain the pasta well and set aside. Pour the soup into the pasta pan over medium heat, then stir in the milk, celery, bell peppers, half the cheese, and the parsley. Add the tuna and gently stir in so that the flakes don't break up. Season to taste with salt and pepper. Heat just until small bubbles appear around the edge of the mixture—do not boil.

4 Stir the pasta into the pan and use 2 forks to mix all the ingredients together. Spoon the mixture into an ovenproof dish and spread out.

5 Stir the remaining cheese into the buttered breadcrumbs, then sprinkle over the top of the pasta mixture. Bake in the preheated oven for 20–25 minutes, until the topping is golden. Let stand for 5 minutes before serving straight from the dish.

macaroni & cheese

Serves 4

Ingredients

2½ cups milk

1 onion, peeled

8 peppercorns

1 bay leaf

4 tbsp butter

scant ⅓ cup all-purpose flour

½ tsp ground nutmeg

⅓ cup heavy cream

scant 1 cup grated sharp cheddar cheese

scant 1 cup crumbled bleu cheese

12 oz/350 g dried macaroni

scant 1 cup grated Gruyère or Emmental cheese

salt and pepper

This is comfort food at its best! For a cheaper version of this dish, use just one type of cheese—a sharp cheddar would be a good choice.

Method

1 Put the milk, onion, peppercorns, and bay leaf in a pan and bring to a boil. Remove from the heat and let stand for 15 minutes.

2 Melt the butter in a pan and stir in the flour until well combined and smooth. Cook over medium heat, stirring constantly, for 1 minute. Remove from the heat. Strain the milk to remove the solids and stir a little into the butter and flour mixture until well incorporated. Return to the heat and gradually add the remaining milk, stirring constantly, until it has all been incorporated. Cook for an additional 3 minutes, or until the sauce is smooth and thickened, then add the nutmeg, cream, and pepper to taste. Add the cheddar and bleu cheeses and stir until melted.

3 Meanwhile, bring a large pan of lightly salted water to a boil. Add the macaroni, return to a boil, and cook for 8–10 minutes, or until just tender. Drain well and add to the cheese sauce. Stir well together.

4 Preheat the broiler to high. Spoon the mixture into an ovenproof dish, then scatter over the Gruyère cheese and cook under the preheated broiler until bubbling and brown.

meatloaf

Serves 6

Ingredients

1 lb/450 g ground beef

9 oz/250 g ground turkey or chicken

9 oz/250 g pork sausages, removed from the casings

2 slices whole wheat bread, made into crumbs

2 eggs, beaten

2 tsp Italian herb seasoning

3 tbsp chopped fresh flat-leaf parsley

12 slices bacon

1 lb 2 oz/500 g bottled strained tomatoes, with added onion

Method

1 Preheat the oven to 350°F/180°C. Put the ground beef and turkey, sausages, breadcrumbs, beaten egg, and herbs into a bowl and mix well using your hands.

2 Line a 9 x 5 x 3-inch/23 x 13 x 8-cm loaf pan with plastic wrap. Put the meat mixture into the pan and press down very well. Invert the pan into a small roasting pan and remove the loaf pan and the plastic wrap. Arrange the bacon slices on top of the meatloaf, cover with foil, and cook in the preheated oven for 1 hour.

3 Heat the strained tomatoes in a small saucepan. Drain off any excess fat from around the meatloaf. Pour the strained tomatoes into the roasting pan and brush over the meatloaf. Return to the oven for 5 minutes. Serve slices of the meatloaf with tomato sauce.

glazed ham steaks

Serves 4

Ingredients

4 ham steaks

4 tbsp brown sugar

2 tsp mustard powder

4 tbsp butter

8 slices canned pineapple, drained

Method

1 Preheat a stovetop grill pan over medium heat. Place the ham steaks on it and cook for 5 minutes, turning once. If you have room for only 2 steaks at a time, cook them completely and keep them warm while cooking the remaining steaks.

2 Combine the brown sugar and mustard in a small bowl.

3 Melt the butter in a large skillet. Add the pineapple and cook for 2 minutes to heat through, turning once. Sprinkle with the sugar-and-mustard mixture and continue cooking over low heat until the sugar has melted and the pineapple is well glazed. Turn the pineapple once more, so that both sides are coated with sauce.

4 Place the ham steaks on individual plates and arrange 2 pineapple slices either next to them or overlapping on top. Spoon over some of the pan juices and serve.

Meat doesn't have to be off the menu when you're cooking on a budget—cheap cuts can be very tasty if cooked correctly.

sausages & mashed potatoes with onion gravy

Serves 4

Ingredients
8 pork sausages
1 tbsp oil

Onion gravy
6 tbsp butter
3 onions, cut in half and sliced
generous 1 cup vegetable stock
salt and pepper

Mashed potatoes
2 lb/900 g starchy potatoes, peeled and cut
  into chunks
4 tbsp butter
3 tbsp hot milk
2 tbsp chopped fresh parsley (optional)
salt and pepper

It pays to buy the best quality sausages you can afford—for a change, try ones with different seasonings. Vegetarians can use veggie sausages in place of the pork sausages.

Method
1 Cook the sausages slowly in a skillet with the oil over low heat. Cover the pan and turn the sausages from time to time. Don't rush the cooking—it will take 25–30 minutes.

2 Meanwhile, make the onion gravy. Melt the butter in a skillet and cook the onions over low heat, stirring constantly, until soft. Continue to cook until they are brown, stirring from time to time. This will take about 30 minutes, but it is worth it because the onions will naturally caramelize. Pour in the stock and simmer until the onion gravy is thick. Season to taste with salt and pepper.

3 To make the mashed potatoes, cook the potatoes in a large pan of salted boiling water for 15–20 minutes. Drain well and mash with a potato masher until smooth. Season to taste with salt and pepper, add the butter, milk, and parsley, if using, and stir well.

4 Serve the sausages with the mashed potatoes and the onion gravy.

boston baked beans

Serves 2

Ingredients
2–4 pork sausages

14 oz/400 g canned white beans, such as cannellini or lima, drained and rinsed

7 oz/200 g bottled strained tomatoes

1 tbsp maple syrup

1 tsp whole grain mustard

4 slices bacon

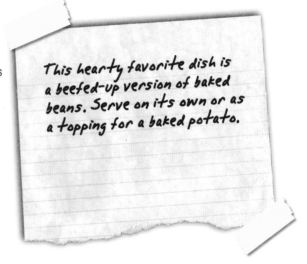

This hearty favorite dish is a beefed-up version of baked beans. Serve on its own or as a topping for a baked potato.

Method
1 Preheat the broiler to high. Cook the sausages under the preheated broiler, turning frequently, for 10–15 minutes, until browned and cooked through.

2 Put the beans, strained tomatoes, maple syrup, and mustard into a pan. Cook gently for about 10 minutes, until heated through.

3 Meanwhile, broil the bacon until crisp and browned. Chop the sausages and add to the beans in the pan. Transfer to serving plates, top with the bacon, and serve immediately.

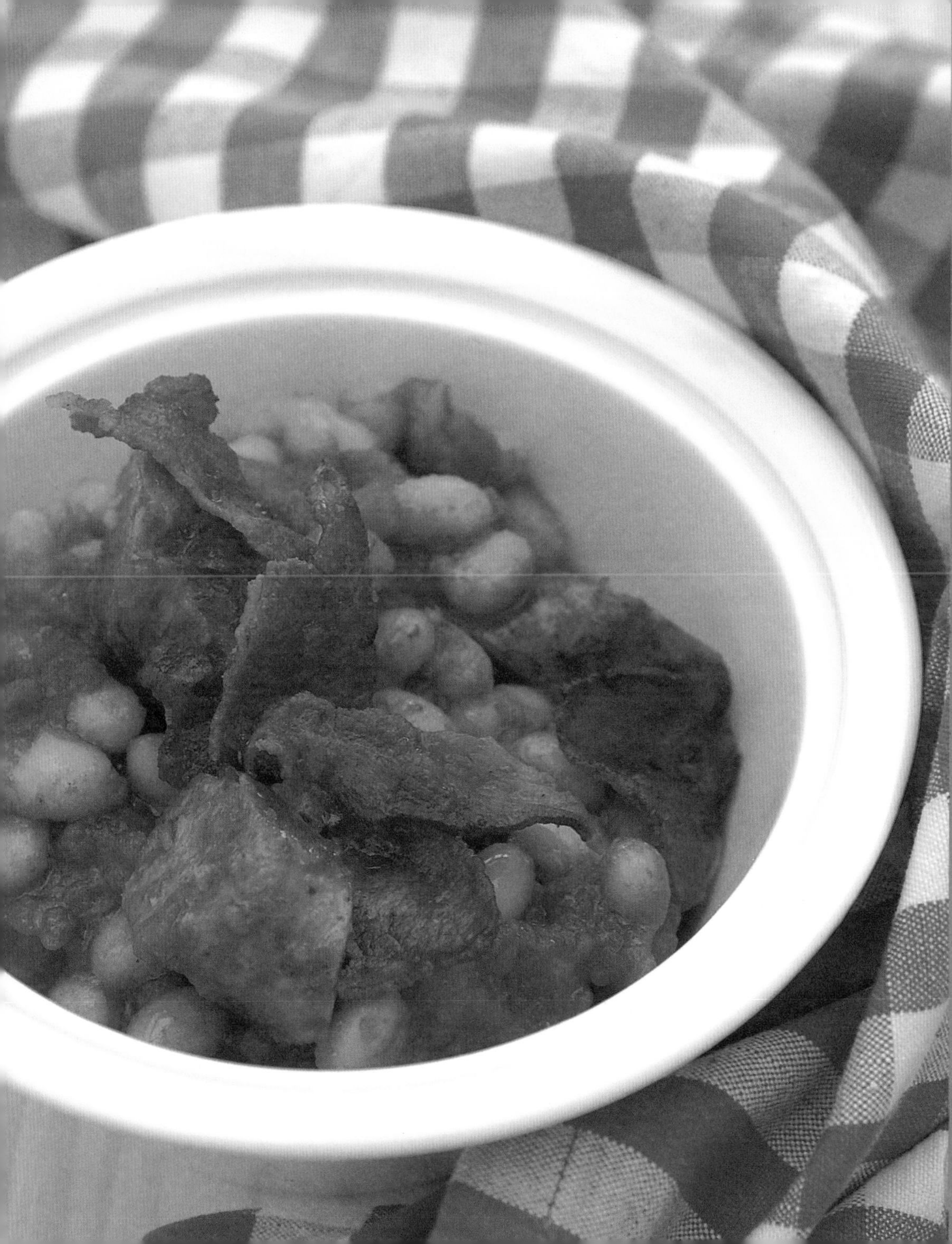

spicy fried eggs

Serves 2

Ingredients

2 tbsp corn oil

1 large onion, finely chopped

2 green or red bell peppers, seeded and coarsely chopped

1 garlic clove, finely chopped

½ tsp dried chile flakes

4 plum tomatoes, peeled and coarsely chopped

2 eggs

1 tbsp chopped fresh flat-leaf parsley (optional)

salt and pepper

Method

1 Heat the oil in a large skillet over medium heat. Add the onion and cook until golden. Add the bell peppers, garlic, and chile flakes, and cook until the bell peppers are softened.

2 Stir in the tomatoes, season to taste with salt and pepper, and simmer over low–medium heat for 10 minutes.

3 Using the back of a spoon, make 2 depressions in the mixture in the skillet. Break the eggs into the depressions, cover, and cook for 3–4 minutes, until the eggs are set. Sprinkle with the parsley, if using, and serve.

bell pepper & mushroom hash

Serves 4

Ingredients

1 lb 8 oz/675 g potatoes, cut into cubes

1 tbsp corn oil

2 garlic cloves, crushed

1 green bell pepper, seeded and cut into cubes

1 yellow bell pepper, seeded and cut into cubes

3 tomatoes, diced

1 cup chopped mushrooms

1 tbsp Worcestershire sauce

2 tbsp chopped fresh basil, plus extra sprigs to garnish

salt and pepper

Method

1 Cook the potatoes in a pan of lightly salted boiling water for 7–8 minutes. Drain well and reserve.

2 Heat the oil in a large skillet. Add the potatoes and cook over medium heat, stirring, for 8–10 minutes, until browned.

3 Add the garlic and bell peppers and cook, stirring frequently, for 2–3 minutes.

4 Add the tomatoes and mushrooms and cook, stirring frequently, for 5–6 minutes.

5 Stir in the Worcestershire sauce and basil and season to taste with salt and pepper. Transfer to a serving dish, garnish with basil sprigs, and serve immediately.

These recipes are packed with vegetables, making them super-healthy but still really tasty!

potato skins with tomato & corn salsa

Serves 2

Ingredients

2 large baking potatoes

oil, for brushing

½ cup grated cheddar cheese

Salsa

3 oz/85 g canned corn kernels

2 oz/55 g canned kidney beans

2 tbsp olive oil

2 tomatoes, seeded and diced

2 shallots, finely sliced

¼ red bell pepper, seeded and finely diced

1 fresh red chile, seeded and finely chopped

1 tbsp chopped fresh cilantro leaves

1 tbsp lime juice

salt and pepper

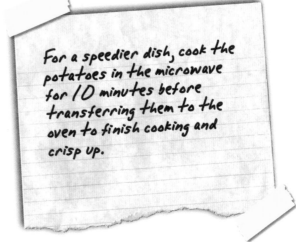

For a speedier dish, cook the potatoes in the microwave for 10 minutes before transferring them to the oven to finish cooking and crisp up.

Method

1 Preheat the oven to 400°F/200°C. Prick the potatoes in several places with a fork and brush with oil. Cook directly on the oven shelf for 1 hour, or until the skins are crispy and the insides are soft when pierced with a fork.

2 Meanwhile, make the salsa. Drain the corn and beans, rinse well, then drain again. Put in a bowl with the oil, tomatoes, shallots, bell pepper, chile, cilantro, lime juice, and salt and pepper to taste and mix well.

3 Preheat the broiler to medium. Cut the potatoes in half lengthwise. Scoop out the flesh, leaving the skins intact. Brush the insides with oil, then put on a baking sheet, cut-sides up. Cook under the preheated broiler for 5 minutes, or until crisp.

4 Spoon the salsa into the potato skins and sprinkle the cheese over the top. Return the filled potato skins to the broiler and cook gently until the cheese has melted. Serve immediately.

beyond the takeout

Sometimes it can be difficult to resist the lure of the takeout, especially if you've had a drink or two. But if you do indulge, you'll soon find that takeout food isn't kind to the wallet, or to the waistline! The recipes in this chapter show how easy it is to make delicious takeout-style food at home at a fraction of the cost and, in many cases, calories. They are perfect for chilled-out nights in or lazy TV dinners.

thai green chicken curry

Serves 4

Ingredients

2 tbsp peanut oil

2 tbsp Thai green curry paste

1 lb 2 oz/500 g skinless, boneless chicken breasts, cut into chunks

2 kaffir lime leaves, torn

1 lemongrass stalk, finely chopped

1 cup coconut milk

2 eggplants, cut into chunks

2 tbsp Thai fish sauce

fresh Thai basil sprigs and thinly sliced kaffir lime leaves, to garnish

> Most Thai ingredients are available in larger supermarkets. However, fresh kaffir lime leaves can be a little tricky to find—you can use dried ones, replace with lime zest, or leave them out altogether.

Method

1 Heat the oil in a preheated wok or large skillet. Add the curry paste and stir-fry briefly until all the aromas are released.

2 Add the chicken, torn lime leaves, and lemongrass and stir-fry for 3–4 minutes, until the meat is beginning to color.

3 Add the coconut milk and eggplants and simmer gently for 8–10 minutes, or until tender.

4 Stir in the fish sauce and serve immediately, garnished with Thai basil sprigs and thinly sliced lime leaves.

vegetable korma

Serves 4

Ingredients

4 tbsp ghee or vegetable oil

2 onions, chopped

2 garlic cloves, chopped

1 fresh red chile, chopped

1 tbsp grated fresh ginger

2 tomatoes, peeled and chopped

1 orange bell pepper, seeded and cut into small pieces

1 large potato, peeled and cut into chunks

1¼ cup cauliflower florets

½ tsp salt

1 tsp ground turmeric

1 tsp ground cumin

1 tsp ground coriander

1 tsp garam masala

scant 1 cup vegetable stock or water

⅔ cup plain yogurt

⅔ cup light cream

4 tbsp chopped fresh cilantro

freshly cooked rice, to serve

> When you add the yogurt and cream in step 5, be careful not to let the mixture come back to a boil—this would cause the yogurt and cream to curdle.

Method

1 Heat the ghee in a large pan over medium heat, add the onions and garlic, and cook, stirring, for 3 minutes.

2 Add the chile and ginger and cook for an additional 4 minutes.

3 Add the tomatoes, bell pepper, potato, cauliflower, salt, and spices and cook, stirring, for an additional 3 minutes.

4 Stir in the stock and bring to a boil. Reduce the heat and simmer for 25 minutes.

5 Stir in the yogurt and cream and cook gently, stirring, for an additional 5 minutes. Add the cilantro and heat through. Serve with rice.

chicken chow mein

Serves 4

Ingredients

9 oz/250 g medium egg noodles

2 tbsp sunflower oil

9 oz/250 g cooked chicken breasts, shredded

1 garlic clove, finely chopped

1 red bell pepper, seeded and thinly sliced

generous 1 cup sliced mushrooms

6 scallions, sliced

1 cup fresh beansprouts

3 tbsp soy sauce

1 tbsp sesame oil

Method

1 Cook the noodles according to the package directions.

2 Heat the sunflower oil in a large preheated wok. Add the chicken, garlic, bell pepper, mushrooms, scallions, and beansprouts to the wok and stir-fry for about 5 minutes.

3 Drain the noodles thoroughly. Add the noodles to the wok, toss well, and stir-fry for an additional 5 minutes.

4 Drizzle the soy sauce and sesame oil over the chow mein and toss until well combined.

5 Transfer to serving bowls and serve immediately.

sesame hot noodles

Serves 6

Ingredients

1 lb 2 oz/500 g dried medium egg noodles

3 tbsp sunflower oil

2 tbsp sesame oil

1 garlic clove, crushed

1 tbsp smooth peanut butter

1 small fresh green chile, seeded and very finely chopped

3 tbsp sesame seeds

4 tbsp light soy sauce

½ tbsp lime juice

4 tbsp chopped fresh cilantro

salt and pepper

Method

1 Cook the noodles according to the package directions.

2 Meanwhile, make the dressing. Mix together the sunflower oil, sesame oil, garlic, and peanut butter in a mixing bowl until smooth.

3 Add the chile, sesame seeds, and soy sauce to the bowl. Add the lime juice and mix well. Season to taste with salt and pepper.

4 Drain the noodles thoroughly, then place in a serving bowl.

5 Add the dressing and cilantro to the noodles and toss well to mix. Serve immediately.

If you don't have a wok, you can use a large skillet or pan instead.

classic stir-fried vegetables

Serves 4

Ingredients

2 tbsp peanut oil

8 scallions, finely chopped

1 garlic clove, crushed

1 tbsp grated fresh ginger

1 head of broccoli, cut into florets

1 orange or yellow bell pepper, seeded and coarsely chopped

1½ cups shredded red cabbage

4½ oz/125 g baby corn

generous 1 cup sliced mushrooms

2¾ cups fresh beansprouts

9 oz/250 g canned water chestnuts, drained

4 tsp soy sauce

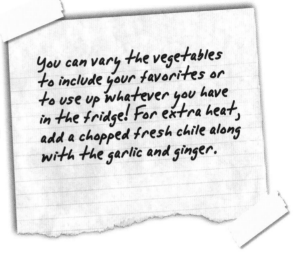

You can vary the vegetables to include your favorites or to use up whatever you have in the fridge! For extra heat, add a chopped fresh chile along with the garlic and ginger.

Method

1 Heat the oil in a large wok over high heat. Stir-fry 6 of the scallions with the garlic and ginger for 30 seconds.

2 Add the broccoli, bell pepper, and red cabbage and stir-fry for 1–2 minutes. Mix in the baby corn and mushrooms and stir-fry for an additional 1–2 minutes.

3 Finally, add the beansprouts and water chestnuts and cook for an additional 2 minutes. Pour in the soy sauce to taste and stir well.

4 Transfer to serving dishes and serve immediately, garnished with the remaining scallions.

chicken skewers with satay sauce

Serves 4

Ingredients

4 skinless chicken breasts, about 5 oz/140 g each

2 tbsp olive oil

2 tbsp lemon juice

Satay sauce

scant ½ cup smooth peanut butter

1½ tbsp olive oil

2 tbsp hot water

1½ tbsp light soy sauce

2 tbsp apple juice

4 tbsp coconut milk

Method

1 To make the satay sauce, mix all the ingredients together in a bowl.

2 If you are using wooden skewers, soak them in cold water for at least 30 minutes. Cut each chicken breast lengthwise into 4 strips and thread each strip onto a presoaked wooden or metal skewer.

3 Mix the oil and lemon juice together in a small bowl, then brush over the chicken.

4 Preheat the broiler to medium–high. Cook the chicken skewers under the preheated broiler for 3 minutes on each side, or until golden and cooked through, making sure that there is no trace of pink inside. Serve the skewers with the sauce.

If you remember, it is a good idea to marinate the meat overnight for extra flavor.

shish kabobs

Serves 4–6

Ingredients

1 lb 2 oz/500 g boneless leg or neck of lamb with a small amount of fat, cut into ¾-inch/2-cm cubes

2 green bell peppers, seeded and cut into ¾-inch/2-cm pieces

1 onion, quartered and separated into layers

8–10 cherry tomatoes

tzatziki and lemon wedges, to serve

Marinade

2 tbsp milk

2 tbsp olive oil, plus extra for brushing

1 large onion, grated

1 tbsp tomato paste

½ tsp ground cumin

salt and pepper

Method

1 To make the marinade, put all the ingredients in a bowl and stir until combined. Add the lamb and mix to coat well with the marinade. Cover and let marinate in the refrigerator for 2 hours. If you are using wooden skewers, soak them in cold water for at least 30 minutes.

2 Preheat the broiler to high. Lightly brush the presoaked wooden or metal skewers with oil, then thread an equal quantity of the lamb cubes onto each one, alternating with pieces of bell pepper, onion layers, and cherry tomatoes.

3 Brush the broiler rack with oil. Add the kabobs and cook, turning frequently and basting with the remaining marinade, for 8–10 minutes, or until the lamb and bell peppers are charred on the edges.

4 Serve the kabobs with tzatziki and lemon wedges.

vegetable chili

Serves 4

Ingredients

1 eggplant, cut into 1-inch/2.5-cm slices

1 tbsp olive oil, plus extra for brushing

1 large red onion, finely chopped

2 red or yellow bell peppers, seeded
and finely chopped

3–4 garlic cloves, finely chopped
or crushed

1 lb 12 oz/800 g canned chopped
tomatoes

1 tbsp mild chili powder

½ tsp ground cumin

½ tsp dried oregano

2 small zucchini, cut lengthwise into
quarters and sliced

14 oz/400 g canned kidney beans, drained
and rinsed

2 cups water

1 tbsp tomato paste

6 scallions, finely chopped

generous 1 cup grated cheddar cheese

salt and pepper

For a hearty supper, serve this veggie chili with freshly cooked rice. Use hot chili powder if you prefer your chili to have a bit of a kick!

Method

1 Brush the eggplant slices on one side with oil. Heat half the oil in a large skillet over medium–high heat. Add the eggplant slices, oiled-side up, and cook for 5–6 minutes, or until browned on one side. Turn the slices over, cook on the other side until browned, and transfer to a plate. Cut into bite-size pieces.

2 Heat the remaining oil in a large pan over medium heat. Add the onion and bell peppers and cook, stirring occasionally, for 3–4 minutes, or until the onion is softened but not browned.

3 Add the garlic and cook for an additional 2–3 minutes, or until the onion is beginning to color.

4 Add the tomatoes, chili powder, cumin, and oregano. Season to taste with salt and pepper. Bring just to a boil, reduce the heat, cover, and simmer gently for 15 minutes.

5 Add the zucchini, eggplant, and kidney beans. Stir in the water and the tomato paste. Return to a boil, then cover and simmer for 45 minutes, or until the vegetables are tender. Ladle into serving bowls and top with the scallions and cheese.

chili con carne

Serves 4

Ingredients

2 tbsp sunflower oil

1 lb 2 oz/500 g ground beef

1 green bell pepper

1 large onion, chopped

1 garlic clove

1 tsp chili powder

1 lb 12 oz/800 g canned chopped tomatoes

1 lb 12 oz/800 g canned red kidney beans, drained and rinsed

2 cups beef stock

handful of fresh cilantro sprigs

salt and pepper

freshly cooked rice and sour cream, to serve

Method

1 Heat the oil in a large pan. Add the beef and cook over medium heat, stirring frequently, for 5 minutes, or until broken up and browned.

2 Seed and dice the bell pepper. Reduce the heat, add the onion, garlic, and bell pepper to the pan, and cook, stirring frequently, for 10 minutes.

3 Stir in the chili powder, tomatoes with their juices, and kidney beans. Pour in the stock and season to taste with salt and pepper. Bring to a boil, reduce the heat, and simmer, stirring frequently, for 15–20 minutes, or until the meat is tender.

4 Chop the cilantro sprigs, reserving a few for a garnish, and stir into the chili. Transfer to serving bowls and garnish with the reserved cilantro sprigs. Serve with rice and sour cream.

Any leftover chili con carne will taste even better the next day.

nachos

Serves 6

Ingredients

6 oz/175 g tortilla chips

14 oz/400 g canned refried beans, warmed

2 tbsp finely chopped canned jalapeño chiles

7 oz/200 g canned pimentos or roasted bell peppers, drained and finely sliced

1 cup grated Gruyère cheese

1 cup grated cheddar cheese

salt and pepper

Method

1 Preheat the oven to 400°F/200°C.

2 Spread the tortilla chips out over the bottom of a large, ovenproof dish or roasting pan. Cover with the warmed refried beans. Sprinkle over the chiles and pimentos and season to taste with salt and pepper. Mix the cheeses together in a bowl and sprinkle on top.

3 Bake in the preheated oven for 5–8 minutes, or until the cheese is bubbling and melted. Serve immediately.

chicken fajitas with guacamole

Serves 4

Ingredients

1 tsp ground cumin

1 tbsp olive oil, plus extra for brushing

1 garlic clove, sliced

juice of 1 lime

4 chicken breasts, about 4 oz/115 g each, cut into strips

4 flour tortillas

1 red bell pepper, seeded and sliced

2 scallions, diagonally sliced

salt and pepper

Guacamole

1 large avocado, halved and pitted

1 garlic clove, crushed

juice of ½ lemon

1 tbsp mayonnaise

salt and pepper

The guacamole will turn brown when exposed to air. To stop this happening, cover with a thin layer of lemon juice or oil.

Method

1 Mix the cumin, oil, garlic, and lime juice together in a nonmetallic, shallow dish. Season the chicken to taste with salt and pepper, then add to the dish and turn to coat in the marinade. Cover with plastic wrap and let marinate in the refrigerator for up to 1 hour, turning the chicken occasionally.

2 To make the guacamole, scoop the flesh from the avocado halves out into a bowl and mash together with the garlic and lemon juice. Add the mayonnaise and salt and pepper to taste and mix until smooth and creamy. Set aside.

3 Preheat a stovetop grill pan. Remove the chicken from the marinade and brush with oil, then cook in the grill pan for 6–8 minutes, turning halfway through the cooking time, until cooked through and golden.

4 Meanwhile, warm the tortillas according to the package directions. Arrange an equal quantity of the chicken, bell pepper, and scallions down the center of each. Add a spoonful of guacamole and roll up. Slice diagonally in half to serve.

STUDENT TASTE TEAM

Name: Chemaine Shehadeh
Studying: Civil Engineering
At: University of Technology, Sydney, Australia
Comments about dish: This was very easy to make

Marks: 8/10

hamburgers

Serves 4

Ingredients

1 lb 10 oz/750 g ground beef

1 beef bouillon cube

1 tbsp minced dried onion

2 tbsp water

½ cup grated cheddar cheese (optional)

4 hamburger buns, split

ketchup, tomato slices, and lettuce leaves, to serve

Method

1 Place the beef in a large mixing bowl. Crumble the bouillon cube over the meat, add the dried onion and water, and mix well. Divide the meat into 4 portions, shape each into a ball, then flatten slightly to make a burger shape of your preferred thickness.

2 Preheat a stovetop grill pan over high heat. Place the burgers on the pan and cook for about 5 minutes on each side, depending on how well done you like your meat and the thickness of the burgers. Press down occasionally with a spatula during cooking.

3 To make cheeseburgers, sprinkle the cheese on top of the burgers after you have turned them.

4 Serve the burgers in buns with ketchup, tomato slices, and lettuce leaves.

If you have time, chill the burgers in the fridge before cooking—this will help them keep their shape.

bean burgers

Serves 6

Ingredients

14 oz/400 g canned cannellini beans, drained and rinsed

2 tbsp red pesto

scant 1½ cups fresh whole wheat breadcrumbs

1 egg

2 tbsp olive oil

½ small red onion, finely chopped

1 garlic clove, crushed

6 whole wheat buns

6 tsp hummus

salt and pepper

tomato slices, cucumber slices, and lettuce leaves, to serve

Method

1 Mash the beans with a potato masher in a bowl until they are smooth, then add the pesto, breadcrumbs, egg, and salt and pepper to taste, and mix well.

2 Heat half the oil in a nonstick skillet over low heat and cook the onion and garlic until soft. Add to the bean mixture and mix well.

3 Heat the remaining oil in the skillet. Spoon in the bean mixture, in 6 separate mounds, then press each one down with the back of a spoon to form a burger.

4 Cook the burgers for 4–5 minutes, then carefully turn over and cook for an additional 4–5 minutes, until golden.

5 Meanwhile, slice the buns in half and spread the bottom half of each with 1 teaspoon of the hummus.

6 Remove the burgers from the skillet and drain on paper towels. Place each one in a bun and serve with tomato slices, cucumber slices, and lettuce leaves.

pizza

Serves 2

Ingredients

Pizza crust

generous 1½ cups white bread flour,
plus extra for dusting

1 tsp active dry yeast

1 tsp salt

2 tbsp olive oil

1–1½ cups warm water

Topping

4 tbsp olive oil

1 large onion, thinly sliced

6 button mushrooms, thinly sliced

½ small green bell pepper, ½ small red bell
pepper, and ½ small yellow bell pepper,
seeded and thinly sliced

10½ oz/300 g store-bought tomato
pizza sauce

2 oz/55 g mozzarella cheese, thickly sliced

2 tbsp freshly grated Parmesan cheese

1 tsp chopped fresh basil

Kneading pizza dough is a great stress-buster! For the best results, you will need to knead the dough for at least 10 minutes. Alternatively, you could use store-bought pizza crusts.

Method

1 Combine the flour, yeast, and salt in a mixing bowl. Drizzle over half the oil. Make a well in the center and pour in the water. Mix to a firm dough and shape into a ball. Turn out onto a floured counter and knead until it is no longer sticky. Oil the bowl with the remaining oil. Put the dough into the bowl and turn to coat with oil. Cover with a dish towel and let rise for 1 hour.

2 When the dough has doubled in size, punch it down to release the excess air, then knead until smooth. Divide in half and roll into 2 thin circles. Place on a baking sheet. Preheat the oven to 425°F/220°C.

3 For the topping, heat the oil in a skillet and cook the onion, mushrooms, and bell peppers for 5 minutes, or until softened. Spread some of the tomato sauce over the pizza crusts, but do not go right to the edge. Top with the vegetables and mozzarella cheese. Spoon over more tomato sauce, then sprinkle with the Parmesan cheese and basil. Bake in the preheated oven for 10 minutes, or until the crusts are crispy and the cheese has melted. Serve immediately.

homemade oven fries

Serves 4

Ingredients

1 lb/450 g potatoes, peeled

2 tbsp corn oil

salt and pepper

Method

1 Preheat the oven to 400°F/200°C.

2 Cut the potatoes into thick, even-size French fries. Rinse them under cold running water and then dry well on a clean dish towel. Put in a bowl, add the oil, and toss together until coated.

3 Spread the fries on a baking sheet and cook in the preheated oven for 40–45 minutes, turning once, until golden. Add salt and pepper to taste and serve hot.

fish cakes

Serves 4

Ingredients

1 lb/450 g potatoes, peeled

1 lb/450 g mixed fish fillets, such as whitefish and salmon, skinned

2 tbsp chopped fresh parsley or tarragon

grated rind of 1 lemon

1 tbsp all-purpose flour

1 egg, beaten

2 cups white or whole wheat breadcrumbs, made from one-day-old bread

4 tbsp vegetable oil

salt and pepper

Method

1 Cut the potatoes into chunks. Cook in a large saucepan of salted boiling water for 15 minutes. Drain well and mash with a potato masher until smooth.

2 Place the fish in a skillet and just cover with water. Bring to a boil over medium heat, then cover and simmer gently for 5 minutes, until just cooked. Remove from the heat and transfer the fish to a plate, draining it well. When cool enough to handle, flake the fish and make sure that there are no bones.

3 Mix the potatoes with the fish, parsley, and lemon rind in a bowl. Season well with salt and pepper and shape into 4 round, flat cakes.

4 Dust the fish cakes with flour, dip them into the beaten egg, then coat thoroughly in the breadcrumbs. Place on a baking sheet and chill in the refrigerator for at least 30 minutes.

5 Heat the oil in the skillet and cook the fish cakes over medium heat for 5 minutes on each side. Use a metal spatula to turn them carefully.

If funds are running low, use canned drained salmon for the fish cakes instead of fresh fish.

chicken nuggets

Serves 4

Ingredients

4 tbsp dry breadcrumbs

2 tbsp grated Parmesan cheese

1 tsp dried thyme

1 tsp salt

pinch of pepper

4 skinless, boneless chicken breasts, cut into cubes

8 tbsp melted butter

barbecue sauce or ketchup, to serve

Method

1 Preheat the oven to 400°F/200°C. Combine the breadcrumbs, cheese, thyme, salt, and pepper on a large, flat plate or in a plastic food bag.

2 Toss the chicken cubes in the melted butter, then in the crumb mixture. Place on a baking sheet and bake in the preheated oven for 10 minutes, until crisp.

3 Remove the chicken nuggets from the oven and serve with barbecue sauce or ketchup.

falafel

Serves 4

Ingredients

1⅓ cups dried chickpeas

1 large onion, finely chopped

1 garlic clove, crushed

2 tbsp chopped fresh flat-leaf parsley, plus extra sprigs to garnish

2 tsp ground cumin

2 tsp ground coriander

½ tsp baking powder

oil, for deep-frying

salt and cayenne pepper

hummus and tomato wedges, to serve

Method

1 Soak the chickpeas overnight in enough cold water to cover them and allow room for expansion. Drain, then place in a pan, cover with fresh water, and bring to a boil. Reduce the heat and let simmer for 1 hour, or until tender. Drain.

2 Place the chickpeas in a food processor and blend to make a coarse paste. Add the onion, garlic, parsley, cumin, coriander, baking powder, and salt and cayenne pepper to taste. Blend again to mix thoroughly.

3 Cover and let rest for 30 minutes, then shape into balls. Let rest for an additional 30 minutes. Heat the oil in a deep-fat fryer or large pan to 350–375°F/180–190°C, or until a cube of bread browns in 30 seconds. Carefully drop in the balls and cook until golden brown. Remove from the oil and drain on paper towels.

4 Garnish with parsley sprigs and serve hot or at room temperature with hummus and tomato wedges.

For falafel in a flash, use canned chickpeas in place of the dried chickpeas.

hummus

Serves 6

Ingredients

1⅔ cups cooked or drained canned chickpeas

⅔ cup tahini, well stirred

⅔ cup olive oil, plus extra for drizzling

2 garlic cloves, coarsely chopped

6 tbsp lemon juice

1 tbsp chopped fresh mint

salt and pepper

paprika, to serve

Method

1 Put the chickpeas, tahini, oil, and ⅔ cup water into the blender and process briefly. Add the garlic, lemon juice, and mint and process until smooth.

2 Check the consistency of the hummus and, if it is too thick, add 1 tablespoon of water and process again. Continue adding water, 1 tablespoon at a time, until the right consistency is achieved. Hummus should have a thick, coating consistency. Season to taste with salt and pepper.

3 Spoon the hummus into a serving dish and drizzle with a little oil. Cover with plastic wrap and chill until required. To serve, dust lightly with paprika.

pita chips

Serves 2

Ingredients

2 whole wheat pitas

olive oil, for brushing

Method

1 Preheat the oven to 350ºF/180ºC. Using a serrated knife, split each pita in half, then quarter each half to make a total of 16 pieces.

2 Place the pieces of pita on a baking sheet, rough-sides up. Lightly brush each piece with oil, then bake in the preheated oven for 20 minutes, or until crisp and golden brown.

3 Let cool completely before serving with dips. These chips will keep fresh in an airtight container for up to 3 days.

paprika chips

Serves 4

Ingredients

2 large potatoes, peeled

3 tbsp olive oil

½ tsp paprika

salt

Method

1 Slice the potatoes very thinly so that they are almost transparent and place in a bowl of cold water, then drain them thoroughly and pat dry with paper towels.

2 Heat the oil in a large skillet and add the paprika. Cook, stirring constantly to ensure that the paprika doesn't catch on the bottom and burn.

3 Add the potato slices to the skillet and cook them in a single layer over low–medium heat for about 5 minutes, or until the potato slices are just beginning to curl slightly at the edges. You may need to do this in batches.

4 Remove the potato slices from the skillet using a slotted spoon and transfer them to paper towels to drain thoroughly.

5 Preheat the broiler to medium. Sprinkle the potato slices with salt and cook under the preheated broiler, turning frequently, for 10 minutes, until they begin to go crisp. Sprinkle with a little more salt and serve immediately.

chocolate popcorn

Serves 2

Ingredients

3 tbsp sunflower oil

⅓ cup popcorn kernels

2 tbsp butter

⅓ cup brown sugar

2 tbsp corn syrup

1 tbsp milk

⅓ cup semisweet chocolate chips

Method

1 Preheat the oven to 300°F/150°C. Heat the oil in a large, heavy-bottom pan. Add the popcorn kernels, cover the pan, and cook, shaking the pan vigorously and frequently, for about 2 minutes, until the popping stops. Turn into a large bowl.

2 Put the butter, sugar, corn syrup, and milk in a pan and heat gently until the butter has melted. Bring to a boil, without stirring, and boil for 2 minutes. Remove from the heat, add the chocolate chips, and stir until melted.

3 Pour the chocolate mixture over the popcorn and toss together until evenly coated. Spread the mixture onto a large baking sheet.

4 Bake in the preheated oven for about 15 minutes, until crisp. Let cool before serving.

131

iced raspberry sundae

Serves 4

Ingredients

generous 2¾ cups fresh raspberries,
plus extra to decorate

2 cups heavy cream

½ cup slivered almonds

1¼ cups fresh pitted or canned cherries

½ oz/15 g semisweet chocolate,
coarsely grated

fresh mint sprigs, to garnish

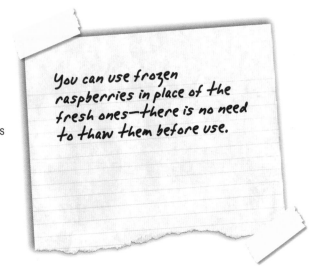

You can use frozen raspberries in place of the fresh ones—there is no need to thaw them before use.

Method

1 Preheat the oven to 400°F/200°C. Set aside ½ cup of the raspberries and lightly crush the remainder.

2 Whip the cream in a bowl until soft peaks form. Put 4 tablespoons of the cream into a small bowl, cover, and set aside. Stir the crushed raspberries into the remaining cream, spoon into a freezerproof container, and freeze for 1 hour, or until partially frozen.

3 Meanwhile, spread the almonds out on a baking sheet and toast in the preheated oven, turning occasionally, for 8–10 minutes, or until golden brown. Remove from the oven and let cool.

4 Arrange the reserved raspberries and the cherries in 4 sundae glasses, then sprinkle with a few toasted almonds. Cover with scoops of the frozen raspberry mixture, then swirl the reserved cream on top. Sprinkle with the grated chocolate and decorate with extra raspberries and mint sprigs.

chocolate ice-cream bites

Serves 6

Ingredients

2½ cups ice cream

7 oz/200 g semisweet chocolate, broken into pieces

2 tbsp unsalted butter

Method

1 Line a baking sheet with plastic wrap.

2 Using a melon baller, scoop out balls of ice cream and place them on the prepared baking sheet. Alternatively, cut the ice cream into bite-size cubes. Stick a toothpick in each piece and return to the freezer until very hard.

3 Place the chocolate and the butter in a heatproof bowl set over a pan of gently simmering water until melted. Quickly dip the frozen ice-cream balls into the warm chocolate and return to the freezer. Keep them there until ready to serve.

fruit skewers

Serves 2

Ingredients

a selection of fruit, such as apricots, peaches, figs, strawberries, mangoes, pineapple, bananas, dates, and papaya, prepared and cut into chunks

2 tbsp maple syrup

1¾ oz/50 g semisweet chocolate, broken into pieces

Method

1 Soak 4 wooden skewers in water for at least 30 minutes.

2 Preheat the broiler to high and line the broiler pan with foil. Thread alternate pieces of fruit onto each skewer. Brush the fruit with the maple syrup.

3 Place the chocolate in a heatproof bowl set over a pan of gently simmering water until melted.

4 Meanwhile, cook the skewers under the preheated broiler for 3 minutes, or until caramelized. Serve drizzled with the melted chocolate.

Semisweet chocolate is a very useful ingredient to have in your kitchen—if you can resist temptation, that is!

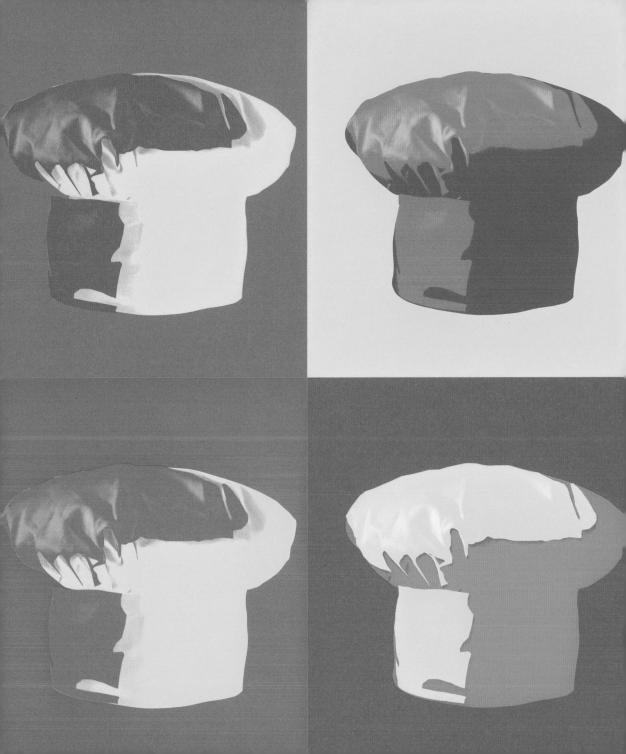

look who's cooking

Once you've been cooking for a while and feel you've mastered the basics, you'll be ready to take on a new challenge—cooking to impress. Whether you want to cook a romantic dinner for a hot date or a first-rate meal for your family or friends, this chapter is packed with ideas for restaurant-style dishes that are sure to fill the bill. Even better, they won't break the bank so you don't need to limit them to special occasions.

spaghetti bolognese

Serves 4

Ingredients

2 tbsp olive oil

1 onion, finely chopped

2 garlic cloves, finely chopped

1 carrot, peeled and finely chopped

1½ cups sliced mushrooms

1 tsp dried oregano

½ tsp dried thyme

1 bay leaf

10 oz/280 g lean ground beef

1¼ cups beef stock

1¼ cups strained tomatoes

12 oz/350 g dried spaghetti

salt and pepper

Method

1 To make the sauce, heat the oil in a heavy-bottom pan. Add the onion and sauté, half covered, for 5 minutes, or until softened. Add the garlic, carrot, and mushrooms and sauté for an additional 3 minutes, stirring occasionally.

2 Add the herbs and ground beef to the pan and cook until the meat has browned, stirring regularly.

3 Add the stock and strained tomatoes. Reduce the heat, season to taste with salt and pepper, and cook over low–medium heat, half covered, for 15–20 minutes, or until the sauce has reduced and thickened. Remove and discard the bay leaf.

4 Meanwhile, bring a large pan of lightly salted water to a boil. Add the pasta, return to a boil, and cook for 8–10 minutes, until tender but still firm to the bite.

5 Drain the pasta, then mix together the pasta and sauce. Serve immediately.

spaghetti with meatballs

Serves 4

Ingredients

⅓ cup fresh breadcrumbs

14 oz/400 g lean ground beef

4 garlic cloves, crushed

1 large egg, lightly beaten

generous ¼ cup grated Parmesan cheese

flour, for coating

2 tbsp olive oil

2 tsp dried oregano

1 lb 12 oz/800 g canned chopped tomatoes

1 tbsp tomato paste

1 tsp sugar

10½ oz/300 g dried spaghetti

salt and pepper

Method

1 Put the breadcrumbs in a large bowl with the beef, half the garlic, the egg, Parmesan cheese, and salt and pepper to taste. Mix well.

2 Flour your hands and roll the mixture into walnut-size balls. Chill the meatballs in the refrigerator while you make the sauce.

3 Heat the oil in a pan and add the remaining garlic and the oregano. Stir for 1 minute. Add the tomatoes, tomato paste, and sugar, bring to a boil, then reduce the heat and simmer for 8 minutes.

4 Carefully place the meatballs in the pan and spoon the sauce over them. Cover and simmer for 20 minutes, turning the meatballs occasionally.

5 Meanwhile, bring a large pan of lightly salted water to a boil. Add the pasta, return to a boil, and cook for 8–10 minutes, until tender but still firm to the bite. Drain the pasta, then serve with the meatballs and sauce.

beef bourguignon

Serves 6

Ingredients

2 tbsp olive oil

6 oz/175 g unsmoked bacon,
   sliced into thin strips

3 lb/1.3 kg braising beef,
   cut into 2-inch/5-cm pieces

2 carrots, peeled and sliced

2 onions, chopped

2 garlic cloves, very finely chopped

3 tbsp all-purpose flour

3 cups red wine

1½–2 cups beef stock

1 bouquet garni

1 tsp salt

¼ tsp pepper

3 tbsp butter

12 oz/350 g pearl onions

12 oz/350 g button mushrooms

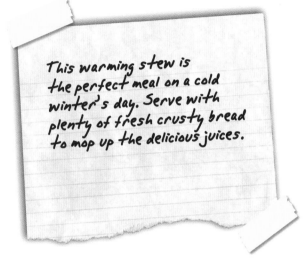

This warming stew is the perfect meal on a cold winter's day. Serve with plenty of fresh crusty bread to mop up the delicious juices.

Method

1 Heat the oil in a large, flameproof casserole over medium heat. Add the bacon and brown for 2–3 minutes. Remove with a slotted spoon. Add the beef in batches to the casserole and cook until browned. Drain and set aside with the bacon.

2 Add the carrots and onions to the casserole and cook for 5 minutes. Add the garlic and cook until just colored. Return the beef and bacon to the casserole. Sprinkle over the flour and cook, stirring, for 1 minute. Add the wine, enough stock to cover, the bouquet garni, salt, and pepper. Bring to a boil, cover, and simmer gently for 3 hours.

3 Heat half the butter in a skillet. Add the pearl onions, cover, and cook until softened. Remove with a slotted spoon and keep warm. Heat the remaining butter in the skillet. Add the mushrooms and cook briefly. Remove and keep warm.

4 Strain the casserole liquid through a strainer into a clean pan. Wipe out the casserole with paper towels and tip the meat mixture back in with the mushrooms and pearl onions. Remove the surface fat from the cooking liquid, simmer for 1–2 minutes to reduce, then pour over the meat and vegetables.

beef goulash

Serves 4

Ingredients

2 tbsp vegetable oil

1 large onion, chopped

1 garlic clove, crushed

1 lb 10 oz/750 g lean braising beef

2 tbsp paprika

14 oz/400 g canned chopped tomatoes

2 tbsp tomato paste

1 large red bell pepper, seeded and
   chopped

2 cups sliced mushrooms

2½ cups beef stock

1 tbsp cornstarch

1 tbsp water

salt and pepper

chopped fresh parsley, to garnish

freshly cooked long-grain and wild rice,
   to serve

Cooking meat in this way makes it so tender that it practically melts in your mouth. Braising beef is very economical and is an ideal choice for anyone who's watching their pennies!

Method

1 Heat the oil in a large, heavy-bottom skillet. Add the onion and garlic and cook over low heat for 3–4 minutes.

2 Using a sharp knife, cut the beef into chunks, add to the skillet, and cook over high heat for 3 minutes, or until browned. Add the paprika and stir well, then add the tomatoes, tomato paste, bell pepper, and mushrooms. Cook for an additional 2 minutes, stirring frequently. Pour in the stock. Bring to a boil, reduce the heat, cover, and simmer for 1¼–2 hours, or until the meat is tender.

3 Blend the cornstarch and water together in a small bowl, then add to the skillet, stirring, until thickened and smooth. Cook for 1 minute. Season to taste with salt and pepper.

4 Transfer the beef goulash to a warmed serving dish, garnish with parsley, and serve with a mix of long-grain and wild rice.

roast chicken

Serves 6

Ingredients

1 chicken, weighing 5 lb/2.25 kg

4 tbsp butter

2 tbsp chopped fresh lemon thyme,
plus extra sprigs to garnish

1 lemon, quartered, plus extra wedges
to garnish

½ cup white wine

salt and pepper

roast potatoes, to serve

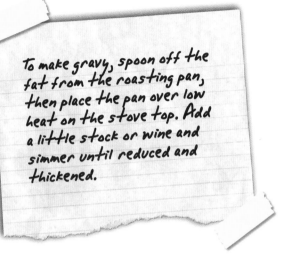

To make gravy, spoon off the fat from the roasting pan, then place the pan over low heat on the stove top. Add a little stock or wine and simmer until reduced and thickened.

Method

1 Preheat the oven to 425°F/220°C. Make sure the chicken is clean, wiping it inside and out using paper towels, and place in a roasting pan.

2 Place the butter in a bowl and soften with a fork, then mix in the chopped thyme and season well with salt and pepper. Butter the chicken all over with the herb butter, inside and out, and place the lemon quarters inside the body cavity. Pour the wine over the chicken.

3 Roast the chicken in the preheated oven for 20 minutes. Reduce the temperature to 375°F/190°C and continue to roast for an additional 1¼ hours, basting frequently. Cover with foil if the skin starts to brown too much.

4 Test that the chicken is cooked by piercing the thickest part of the leg with a sharp knife or skewer and making sure the juices run clear.

5 Remove the chicken from the roasting pan and place on a warmed serving plate to rest, covered with foil, for 10 minutes before carving.

6 Serve with roast potatoes and gravy (see above), garnished with thyme sprigs and lemon wedges.

southern fried chicken

Serves 4–6

Ingredients

1 chicken, weighing 3 lb 5 oz/1.5 kg,
    cut into 6 or 8 pieces

½ cup all-purpose flour

2–4 tbsp butter

corn or peanut oil, for shallow-frying

salt and pepper

Buying a whole chicken and cutting it up yourself (or asking your butcher to do it) is usually cheaper than buying chicken portions. This dish could also be made using chicken drumsticks.

Method

1. Put the chicken into a large bowl with 1 teaspoon of salt and enough water to cover, then cover the bowl and let stand in the refrigerator for at least 4 hours, but ideally overnight. Drain the chicken pieces well and pat completely dry with paper towels.

2. Put the flour and salt and pepper to taste into a plastic bag. Add the chicken pieces and shake until well coated. Remove the chicken pieces from the bag and shake off any excess flour.

3. Melt 2 tablespoons of the butter with about ½ inch/ 1 cm of oil in a flameproof casserole or large skillet with a lid over medium–high heat.

4. Add as many chicken pieces as will fit in a single layer without overcrowding, skin-side down. Cook for 5 minutes, or until the skin is golden and crisp. Turn the chicken over and cook for an additional 10–15 minutes, covered, until the juices run clear when a skewer is inserted into the thickest part of the meat. Remove the chicken from the casserole and drain well on paper towels. Keep warm while cooking any remaining chicken, adding more butter and oil if necessary. Serve hot or cold.

paella

Serves 2–3

Ingredients

2 tbsp olive oil

1 onion, diced

2 skinless chicken breasts, sliced

1 small red bell pepper, seeded and diced

2 garlic cloves, chopped

1 tomato, seeded and chopped

1 tbsp tomato paste

½ tsp turmeric

2½ cups chicken or vegetable stock

scant 1 cup paella rice

½ cup frozen peas

4 oz/115 g cooked shrimp,
   thawed if frozen

salt and pepper

> Do not stir the paella during cooking, but shake the pan once or twice. The paella is ready when you smell a faint toasty aroma coming from the rice. If you're feeling well-off, use saffron instead of the turmeric for a more authentic flavor.

Method

1. Heat the oil in a large, heavy-bottom skillet with a lid. Add the onion and fry for 5 minutes, or until softened. Add the chicken, bell pepper, and garlic and sauté for 5 minutes over medium heat, stirring frequently to prevent the mixture from sticking.

2. Add the tomato, tomato paste, turmeric, and stock to the skillet. Stir in the rice and bring to a boil, then reduce the heat and simmer, covered, for 15 minutes, or until the rice is tender.

3. Add the peas, shrimp, and salt and pepper to taste and cook for an additional 2–3 minutes, or until the shrimp have heated through.

beef lasagna with ricotta

Serves 6

Ingredients

¾ cup olive oil

4 tbsp butter

½ cup diced bacon

1 onion, finely chopped

1 celery stalk, finely chopped

1 carrot, peeled and finely chopped

12 oz/350 g beef pot roast in a single piece

5 tbsp red wine

2 tbsp sun-dried tomato paste

7 oz/200 g Italian sausage

2 eggs

1⅓ cups grated Parmesan cheese

½ cup fresh breadcrumbs

1½ cups ricotta cheese

8 dried no-precook lasagna sheets

12 oz/350 g mozzarella cheese, sliced

salt and pepper

chopped fresh parsley, to garnish (optional)

Method

1 Heat ½ cup of the oil with the butter in a large pan. Add the bacon, onion, celery, and carrot and cook over low heat, stirring occasionally, for 5 minutes, until softened. Increase the heat to medium, add the beef, and cook until evenly browned. Stir in the wine and tomato paste, season to taste with salt and pepper, and bring just to a boil. Reduce the heat, cover, and simmer very gently, stirring occasionally, for 1½ hours, until the beef is tender.

2 Meanwhile, heat 2 tablespoons of the remaining oil in a skillet. Add the sausage and cook, turning frequently, for 8–10 minutes. Remove from the skillet and remove and discard the skin. Thinly slice the sausage and set aside.

3 Transfer the beef to a cutting board and dice finely. Return half the beef to the sauce. Mix the remaining beef with 1 egg, 1 tablespoon of the Parmesan, and the breadcrumbs. Shape into walnut-size balls. Heat the remaining oil in a skillet. Cook the meatballs, turning frequently, for 5–8 minutes, until browned.

4 Pass the ricotta through a strainer into a bowl. Stir in the remaining egg and 4 tablespoons of the remaining Parmesan.

5 Preheat the oven to 350°F/180°C. In a rectangular, ovenproof dish, make layers of lasagna sheets, ricotta mixture, meat sauce, meatballs, sausage, and mozzarella. Finish with a layer of the ricotta mixture and sprinkle with the remaining Parmesan.

6 Bake in the preheated oven for 20–25 minutes, or until golden brown. Remove from the oven, garnish with parsley, if using, and serve.

If using regular dried lasagna, you will need to cook it according to the package directions before use.

risotto

Serves 4

Ingredients

8 cups vegetable stock or water

1 tbsp olive oil

3 tbsp butter

1 small onion, finely chopped

1 lb/450 g arborio rice

½ cup grated Parmesan cheese, plus extra
    shavings to garnish

salt and pepper

Method

1 Bring the stock to a boil, then reduce the heat and
   keep simmering gently over low heat while you are
   cooking the risotto. Heat the oil with 2 tablespoons
   of the butter in a deep pan over medium heat until
   the butter has melted. Stir in the onion and cook
   gently until softened.

2 Add the rice and mix to coat in the oil and butter.
   Cook and stir for 2–3 minutes, or until the grains
   are translucent. Gradually add the stock, a ladleful
   at a time. Stir constantly and add more liquid as
   the rice absorbs it. Cook for 20 minutes, or until all
   the liquid is absorbed. The risotto should be of a
   creamy consistency with a bit of bite in the rice.

3 Remove the risotto from the heat and add the
   remaining butter. Mix well, then stir in the grated
   Parmesan and season to taste with salt and pepper.
   Serve with Parmesan shavings.

pasta with fresh pesto

Serves 4

Ingredients

about 40 fresh basil leaves

3 garlic cloves, crushed

2 tbsp pine nuts

scant ½ cup grated Parmesan cheese,
    plus extra to serve

2–3 tbsp extra virgin olive oil

12 oz/350 g dried pasta

salt and pepper

Method

1 Rinse the basil leaves and pat them dry with
   paper towels.

2 Place the basil leaves, garlic, pine nuts, and
   Parmesan cheese in a tall beaker and process
   using a handheld stick blender for 30 seconds,
   or until smooth. Alternatively, pound all of the
   ingredients by hand, using a mortar and pestle.

3 Gradually add the oil, stirring constantly, then
   season to taste with salt and pepper.

4 Bring a large pan of lightly salted water to a
   boil. Add the pasta, return to a boil, and cook for
   8–10 minutes, until tender but still firm to the
   bite. Drain the pasta thoroughly, then transfer
   to a serving plate and add the pesto. Toss to
   mix well and serve immediately, sprinkled with
   extra Parmesan.

*This basic risotto recipe is
infinitely versatile—just add
your favorite ingredients
to create your own special
version.*

stuffed bell peppers with basil

Serves 4

Ingredients

5 oz/140 g long-grain white or brown rice

4 large red bell peppers

2 tbsp olive oil

1 garlic clove, chopped

4 shallots, chopped

1 celery stalk, chopped

3 tbsp chopped toasted walnuts

2 tomatoes, peeled and chopped

1 tbsp lemon juice

⅓ cup raisins

4 tbsp grated cheddar cheese

2 tbsp chopped fresh basil

salt and pepper

You can use leftover cooked rice for this recipe. Try experimenting with different flavors, varying the nuts, dried fruit, cheese, and herbs according to what you have to hand.

STUDENT TASTE TEAM

Name: Anthony Trigo
Studying: History
At: Royal Holloway, London, UK
Comments about dish: This recipe was easy to make

Marks: 7/10

Method

1 Preheat the oven to 350°F/180°C. Cook the rice in a pan of lightly salted boiling water for 20 minutes if using white rice, or 35 minutes if using brown. Drain, rinse under cold running water, then drain again.

2 Using a sharp knife, cut the tops off the bell peppers and set aside. Remove the seeds and white cores, then blanch the bell peppers and reserved tops in boiling water for 2 minutes. Remove from the heat and drain well.

3 Heat half the oil in a large skillet. Add the garlic and shallots and cook, stirring, for 3 minutes. Add the celery, walnuts, tomatoes, lemon juice, and raisins and cook for an additional 5 minutes. Remove from the heat and stir in the rice, cheese, and basil. Season to taste with salt and pepper.

4 Stuff the bell peppers with the rice mixture and arrange them in a baking dish. Place the tops on the bell peppers, drizzle over the remaining oil, loosely cover with foil, and bake in the preheated oven for 45 minutes. Serve immediately.

perfect roast potatoes

Serves 6

Ingredients

3 lb/1.3 kg large starchy potatoes, peeled and cut into even-size chunks

3 tbsp dripping, goose fat, duck fat, or oil

salt

Method

1 Preheat the oven to 425°F/220°C.

2 Cook the potatoes in a large pan of lightly salted boiling water, covered, for 5–7 minutes. They will still be firm. Meanwhile, add the fat to a roasting pan and place in the preheated oven.

3 Drain the potatoes well and return them to the pan. Cover with the lid and firmly shake the pan so that the surface of the potatoes is slightly roughened.

4 Remove the roasting pan from the oven and carefully tip the potatoes into the hot fat. Baste them to make sure that they are all coated with it.

5 Roast the potatoes at the top of the oven for 45–50 minutes, turning once, until they are browned all over.

6 Sprinkle with a little salt and serve immediately.

garlic mashed potatoes

Serves 4

Ingredients

2 lb/900 g starchy potatoes, peeled and cut into chunks

8 garlic cloves, crushed

¾ cup milk

6 tbsp butter

pinch of ground nutmeg

salt and pepper

1 tbsp chopped fresh flat-leaf parsley, to garnish

Method

1 Cook the potatoes in a large pan of lightly salted boiling water for 10 minutes. Add the garlic and cook for an additional 10–15 minutes, until the potatoes are tender.

2 Drain the potatoes and garlic thoroughly, reserving 3 tablespoons of the cooking liquid.

3 Return the reserved liquid to the pan, add the milk, and bring to simmering point. Add the butter and return the potatoes and garlic to the pan. Mash thoroughly with a potato masher.

4 Season to taste with nutmeg, salt, and pepper and beat with a wooden spoon until light and fluffy. Garnish with parsley and serve immediately.

vegetable rösti

Serves 4

Ingredients

1 carrot, peeled and grated

1 zucchini, grated

1 sweet potato, peeled and grated

8 scallions, finely chopped or shredded

1 egg white, beaten

2 tsp corn oil

pepper

Method

1 Mix all the vegetables together and season with pepper to taste, then stir in the egg white. Using clean hands, form into 8 small patties. Press them firmly together.

2 Heat the oil in a nonstick skillet and cook the patties, in batches, over low heat for 3–4 minutes on each side, or until golden.

cauliflower in cheese sauce

Serves 4

Ingredients

1 head of cauliflower, broken into florets

3 tbsp butter

¼ cup all-purpose flour

scant 2 cups milk

1 cup grated cheddar cheese

pinch of ground nutmeg

1 tbsp grated Parmesan cheese

salt and pepper

Method

1 Cook the cauliflower in a large pan of lightly salted boiling water for 3 minutes. Drain and transfer to an ovenproof dish.

2 Melt the butter in a pan over medium heat and stir in the flour. Cook for 1 minute, stirring constantly, then remove from the heat and gradually add the milk, stirring until smooth. Return to a low heat, bring to a boil, and simmer until the sauce has thickened. Stir in the cheddar and nutmeg. Season to taste with salt and pepper.

3 Preheat the broiler. Pour the cheese sauce over the cauliflower, sprinkle over the Parmesan, and cook under the preheated broiler until browned.

crumble

Serves 6

Ingredients
1 lb/450 g baking apples
1 lb/450 g blackberries
generous ½ cup superfine sugar
4 tbsp water

Crumble topping
1½ cups whole wheat flour
6 tbsp unsalted butter
⅓ cup soft brown sugar
1 tsp apple pie spice

Method
1 Preheat the oven to 375°F/190°C. Prepare the apples by cutting them into quarters, then peeling, and coring them. Thinly slice them into an ovenproof dish. Add the blackberries and then stir in the superfine sugar. Pour in the water.

2 Make the crumble topping by placing the flour in a mixing bowl and rubbing in the butter until the mixture resembles breadcrumbs. Stir in the brown sugar and apple pie spice. Spread the topping evenly over the fruit and press down lightly.

3 Put the dish on a baking sheet and bake in the center of the preheated oven for 25–30 minutes, until the topping is golden brown.

This simple crumble recipe is easily adapted to include different fruits.

banana fritters

Serves 4

Ingredients
½ cup all-purpose flour
2 tbsp rice flour
1 tbsp superfine sugar
1 egg, separated
⅔ cup coconut milk
sunflower oil, for deep-frying
4 large bananas, peeled

To serve
1 tsp confectioners' sugar
1 tsp ground cinnamon
lime wedges

Method
1 Sift the all-purpose flour, rice flour, and superfine sugar into a bowl and make a well in the center. Add the egg yolk and coconut milk. Beat the mixture until a smooth, thick batter forms.

2 Whisk the egg white in a clean, dry bowl until stiff enough to hold soft peaks. Fold it into the batter lightly and evenly.

3 Heat 2½ inches/6 cm of oil in a deep-fat fryer or a large saucepan to 350–375°F/180–190°C, or until a cube of bread browns in 30 seconds. Cut the bananas in half crosswise, then dip them quickly into the batter to coat them.

4 Drop the bananas carefully into the hot oil and deep-fry in batches for 2–3 minutes, until golden brown, turning once.

5 Drain on paper towels. Sprinkle with confectioners' sugar and cinnamon and serve immediately with lime wedges for squeezing over.

creamy rice pudding

Serves 4

Ingredients
butter, for greasing
½ cup golden raisins,
   plus extra to decorate
5 tbsp superfine sugar
3¼ oz/90 g sweet rice
5 cups milk
1 tsp vanilla extract
finely grated rind of 1 large lemon
pinch of ground nutmeg
chopped pistachios, to decorate

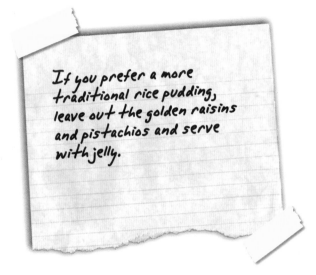

If you prefer a more traditional rice pudding, leave out the golden raisins and pistachios and serve with jelly.

Method
1 Preheat the oven to 325°F/160°C. Grease a 3½-cup/850-ml ovenproof dish.

2 Put the golden raisins, sugar, and rice into a mixing bowl, then stir in the milk and vanilla extract. Transfer to the prepared dish, sprinkle over the grated lemon rind and the nutmeg, then bake in the preheated oven for 2½ hours.

3 Remove from the oven and transfer to individual serving bowls. Decorate with golden raisins and chopped pistachios and serve.

chocolate mousse

Serves 4

Ingredients

10½ oz/300 g semisweet chocolate

1½ tbsp unsalted butter

1 tbsp brandy

4 eggs, separated

Method

1 Break the chocolate into small pieces and place in a heatproof bowl set over a pan of gently simmering water. Add the butter and melt with the chocolate, stirring, until smooth. Remove from the heat, stir in the brandy, and let cool slightly. Add the egg yolks and beat until smooth.

2 In a separate bowl, whisk the egg whites until stiff peaks have formed, then fold them into the chocolate mixture. Spoon the mixture into 4 small serving bowls and level the surfaces. Transfer to the refrigerator and chill for at least 4 hours, until set.

quick tiramisu

Serves 4

Ingredients

1 cup mascarpone cheese or cream cheese

1 egg, separated

2 tbsp plain yogurt

2 tbsp superfine sugar

2 tbsp dark rum

2 tbsp cold strong black coffee

8 ladyfingers

2 tbsp grated semisweet chocolate

Method

1 Put the mascarpone cheese, egg yolk, and yogurt in a large bowl and beat together until smooth.

2 Whisk the egg white in a separate bowl until stiff but not dry, then whisk in the sugar and gently fold into the cheese mixture. Divide half the mixture among 4 sundae glasses.

3 Mix the rum and coffee together in a shallow dish. Dip the ladyfingers briefly into the rum mixture, break them in half, or into smaller pieces if necessary, and divide among the glasses.

4 Stir any remaining coffee mixture into the remaining cheese mixture and divide among the glasses.

5 Sprinkle with the grated chocolate. Serve immediately or cover and chill in the refrigerator until required.

Eating raw eggs should be avoided by infants, the elderly, pregnant women, convalescents, and anyone with a chronic condition.

useful
stuff

If you are new to cooking, you might discover that there are techniques and equipment mentioned in recipes that you are unfamiliar with. You may find yourself asking "What's the difference between *boiling* and *simmering*?" or "What on earth is a *mortar and pestle*?". Well, this section has the answers to those questions and many more. It will increase your understanding of *cooking jargon* and help you onto the path to becoming an experienced and knowledgeable cook.

PREPARATION TECHNIQUES

This section, arranged in handy alphabetical order, is a valuable source of reference for all the preparation techniques you are likely to find in everyday cooking.

Baste

When you spoon juices or fat over a food during cooking, this is known as "basting." It helps to keep the food moist and seal in the flavor.

Beat

This technique involves using a fork, spoon, or electric mixer in a vigorous stirring motion to remove any lumps from sauces and incorporate air.

Blend

Blending involves combining two or more ingredients together by stirring with a spoon or pureeing with an electric blender.

Chop

This means to cut food into small pieces using a sharp knife. You can chop food coarsely or finely depending on the dish you are cooking. Coarsely chopped means that the food will be left in larger pieces than when finely chopped.

Cream

Creaming is similar to beating in that you use a fork, spoon, or electric mixer to beat ingredients together until they are smooth. This technique is usually associated with ingredients that are rich and creamy, such as butter.

Crush

This technique is useful for bringing out the flavor of garlic and herbs, and can be done by pressing the flat side of a knife blade down onto the garlic or herbs.

Cut

This method means to use a sharp knife to make an incision or separate a food into smaller pieces.

Dice

This means to cut food into small cubes using a sharp knife.

Fold

This technique involves mixing a light mixture into a heavier one slowly and gently using a spoon or spatula in a figure-of-eight movement. This is done to keep the air in the mixture.

Grate

To shred food into small pieces using a grater.

Grease/Oil

This is to rub a little butter or oil over the surface of a pan to prevent food from sticking to it during cooking.

Grind

To crush food, such as nuts or spices, to a powder or into very small pieces. You can use a pestle and mortar for a coarser result, or a coffee grinder or food processor.

Julienne

This technique involves cutting food, such as carrots and celery, into fine batons or strips.

Knead

This technique uses the heel of the hand to pull and stretch bread dough in order to develop the gluten in the flour so that the bread will keep its shape when it has risen.

Knock back

This means to knock the air out of bread dough after it has risen.

Marinate

This term means to soak food in a marinade in order to tenderize it and give it more flavor. You can marinate meat, poultry, fish, and vegetables.

Mash

Mashing means to reduce food, often cooked potatoes or other root vegetables, to a pulp using a potato masher or fork.

Peel

Peeling involves removing the outer skin or rind from foods, such as oranges, avocados, or potatoes. Depending on the food, you can use your hands, a sharp knife, or a vegetable peeler.

Puree

This describes reducing food to a smooth pulp. You can do this by pushing food through a strainer or using a blender.

Rub in

This technique is mainly used in making pastry. Using the fingertips, rub the fat into the flour, lifting it high over the bowl in order to trap air into the mixture.

Score

This term means to make light incisions on the surface of a food, especially meat, poultry, or fish, in order to facilitate cooking, let any fat drain, and create a decorative effect.

Shred

This technique involves using a small, sharp knife or grater to cut food into very thin lengths.

Sift

This technique involves shaking dry ingredients, such as flour, through a strainer or sifter to remove lumps and introduce air into the mixture.

Snip

This means to use kitchen shears to cut leafy green vegetables or herbs into very small pieces.

Whisk

Whisking involves beating a light mixture, such as cream or eggs, vigorously with a whisk to incorporate more air. You can use a wire whisk, an electric hand mixer, or a food processor with a whisk attachment.

Zest

This means to remove the outer layer of citrus fruit. A zester takes off the zest without picking up the bitter white pith underneath.

COOKING METHODS

From traditional cooking techniques, such as boiling and roasting, to more contemporary ones, like steaming and stir-frying, there are many different ways to cook food. This section summarizes some of the most popular ones.

Bake

This technique involves cooking food in an oven using dry heat.

Blanch

To plunge a food into boiling water for a few minutes, then remove and place in ice water. This technique is often used to preserve the color and texture of vegetables, and to loosen the skins of tomatoes.

Boil

This means to cook food in a liquid (usually water, stock, or milk) in a saucepan at boiling point (212°F/100°C). Not all foods are boiled continuously—sometimes they are "brought to a boil," then the temperature is reduced and the food is left to simmer. This method is also used to "reduce" a liquid or sauce (i.e. to evaporate off any excess moisture and make the sauce thicker).

Braise

This is a long, slow way to cook food and is especially useful for tough cuts of meat. To braise foods, first brown them in oil, then cook them very slowly in a small amount of flavored liquid in a pan or casserole dish with a tight-fitting lid. You can cook them on the stove top or in the oven.

Broil

Broiling food involves cooking it directly under the heat source.

Deep-fry

This involves immersing food completely in very hot oil and cooking it at a very high temperature. It can be dangerous as it is possible to spill the hot oil or the pan can catch fire, so great care must be taken and the pan should never be left unattended. A thermostatically-controlled deep-fat fryer is a safer and easier option, but this still needs care and attention during use.

Grill

Grilling food means to cook it over a heat source, for example in a stovetop grill pan or over a barbecue.

Dry-fry

This means to cook food, such as nuts or spices, without using fat or oil to color it lightly.

Poach

Poaching means to cook food in a liquid at just below boiling point. You can poach poultry, fish, eggs, and fruit.

Roast

Roasting is similar to baking, in that a food is cooked in the oven using dry heat, and is often used for meat, poultry, and vegetables. It is usually necessary to add a little fat when roasting foods to keep them moist.

Sauté

This is similar to shallow-frying, but with less oil. It also involves moving the food around to prevent it from browning too quickly.

Shallow-fry

This method uses less oil than deep-frying and is suitable for foods that will not burn easily—for example, foods that are coated in flour, breadcrumbs, or batter. The food is not moved around the pan during cooking, but may be turned over halfway through.

Simmer

To simmer means to cook food in liquid that is just below boiling point—there will be very gentle bubbles on the surface of the liquid.

Steam

This means to cook a food with steam, either using a metal or bamboo steamer placed inside a pan containing a small amount of water or an electric steamer. It is a very healthy cooking method because the food doesn't come into contact with the liquid and therefore more of the nutrients are preserved.

Stir-fry

This originated in Asia and is a quick and healthy method of cooking. Foods, such as meat, poultry, and vegetables, are cut into small, even-size pieces and cooked quickly in a little hot oil, while being tossed constantly. You can use a wok or a large skillet for stir-frying, but a wok is better because its shape means that the food is cooked more rapidly as it comes into contact with the hot sides of the wok.

TABLE OF EQUIVALENTS

Oven Temperatures

°F	°C
225	110
250	120
275	140
300	150
325	160
350	180
375	190
400	200
425	220
450	230
475	240

Liquid Measures

1 teaspoon (tsp)	4.6207 milliliters (ml)
1 tablespoon (tbsp)	18.4829 milliliters
1 cup	8 fluid ounces (fl oz)
1 quart	32 fluid ounces

Dry Measures

1 ounce (oz)	28 grams (g)
1 pound (lb)	454 grams
2.2046 pounds	1 kilogram (kg)

Length

0.0394 inch (in)	1 millimeter (mm)
0.3937 inch	1 centimeter (cm)
1 inch	2.54 cm

EQUIPMENT

You may find that your student kitchen is already equipped with a range of basic utensils or, on the other hand, you might not be that lucky. Either way, it's worth having a few carefully chosen kitchen tools of your own that you can take with you when you move on to new accommodation. When you are starting out, you can make do with a few multipurpose utensils, then add to them as your confidence and repertoire grow.

Baking dish

An ovenproof dish, often ceramic, that is used for cooking food in the oven.

Baking sheets

These are flat metal sheets, sometimes with a rim around the edges. They are essential for baking a variety of foods.

Bottle opener/Corkscrew

Essential for opening bottles of wine or beer, you can buy these individually or combined into one utensil.

Cake pans

A cake pan is an essential item if you want to bake a cake. Always use the size specified in the recipe.

Can opener

Although many tins and cans now come with handy ring pulls, this is a useful tool to have in your kitchen drawer.

Casserole dish

This is handy for cooking casseroles, pot-roasts, and stews in the oven. A flameproof casserole may also be used over direct heat on the stove top to brown food before being transferred to the oven.

Colander

A colander is a perforated bowl that is used for draining liquid from foods, such as pasta.

Cutting boards

Essential for protecting the work surface when you are cutting foods, these are available in a range of different materials. Ideally, you should keep a separate board for raw meat and poultry.

Deep-fat fryer

This machine is used for deep-frying foods, such as fries. It is safer than deep-frying using a saucepan as it regulates the temperature of the oil, but should still be used with great care and never left unattended.

Garlic press

This utensil is used for crushing garlic cloves cleanly and efficiently. If you don't have one, you can crush garlic by pressing down on the garlic clove with the side of a heavy knife.

Grater

This is used for shredding foods, such as cheese, vegetables, and chocolate. A hollow box-shape grater is a good multipurpose tool as it has different-size cutting holes on each side, allowing you to grate finely or coarsely depending on the recipe.

Grill pan

Although not essential, a ridged, stovetop grill pan gives food a lovely stripy effect and is ideal for cooking steaks.

Handheld stick blender

This electrical item is a portable version of a blender and allows you to puree foods, such as soups, in the saucepan, saving on washing up. It is also useful for making smoothies and dips.

Kitchen shears

Shears have all sorts of uses in the kitchen—for example, they are handy for chopping meat into small pieces and for snipping herbs. Choose stainless-steel all-purpose shears and keep them especially for use in the kitchen.

Knives

There is a huge range of different knives available. For everyday cooking, a small paring knife, a long cook's knife, and a long, serrated bread knife should be adequate.

Lemon squeezer

This is used for extracting the juice from citrus fruits, such as lemons and limes. The most common type has a cone onto which you press the halved fruit and a bowl to catch the juice. Some have a built-in strainer to catch the pips.

Measuring cups

Liquid measuring cups are made out of clear glass or plastic and have markers printed up the sides. When checking a measurement, place the measuring cup on a flat surface at eye level.

Dry measuring cups come in increments of $\frac{1}{4}$, $\frac{1}{3}$, $\frac{1}{2}$, $\frac{2}{3}$, $\frac{3}{4}$, and 1 cup and are used to measure dry ingredients and soft solids, such as butter. To use, spoon the ingredient into the appropriate cup and level off the excess with the straight edge of a knife.

Measuring spoons

These spoons are ideal for measuring both liquid and dry ingredients accurately. For everyday cooking, you can use ordinary kitchen spoons but be aware that they can vary in size quite substantially.

Mixing bowls

Mixing bowls are available in a variety of materials. It is useful to have at least one large and one small.

Pastry brush

Pastry brushes are handy for brushing glazes onto foods. They can also be used for greasing and oiling bakeware to prevent food from sticking during cooking.

Pestle and mortar

These two utensils come as a pair—the bowl is called the mortar and stick is the pestle. They are used for grinding foods, such as nuts and spices.

Potato masher

This utensil is used for crushing potatoes and other root vegetables until they are smooth.

Roasting pans

These metal pans are deeper than baking sheets, and are ideal for roasting meat and poultry.

Saucepans

Saucepans are used for cooking foods over direct heat on the stove top. It is good to have them in a variety of sizes so you have a suitable one for each different job. Choose saucepans with well-fitting lids.

Skewers

These are long metal or wooden sticks that are used to skewer meats and other ingredients to make kabobs. Wooden skewers should be soaked before use to stop them burning.

Skillet

This is like a saucepan, only shallower. A small skillet is useful for cooking omelets, while a large one can be used for more substantial foods.

Slotted spoon

This is a large spoon with holes or slots in it. It is ideal for lifting foods out of liquids so that the liquid drains away.

Strainer

Like colanders, strainers are used for draining foods, although their holes are much finer than those on a colander. Strainers are useful for sifting flour to remove lumps.

Timer

A kitchen timer is handy for monitoring cooking times and will sound an alarm when the time is up. Most wristwatches have a timer function.

Tongs

A set of tongs is perfect for gripping and turning hot foods.

Vegetable peeler

You can peel vegetables or fruit with a knife, but vegetable peelers make the job easier and safer. There are various different styles of vegetable peeler, from swivel-blade to Y-shape.

Whisk

Wire whisks are useful for whisking ingredients, such as cream, to incorporate air into them. If you don't have one, you can use a fork or a spoon but it will take a lot longer.

Wire cooling racks

These metal racks are used to let air circulate around baked goods, such as cookies and cakes, as they cool so that they don't become soggy.

Wok

A large, bowl-shape pan used in Asian cuisine, the wok's curved sides make it perfect for stir-frying. If you don't have one, a deep skillet or large saucepan can be used instead.

Wooden spoon

Wooden spoons are used for mixing ingredients together. They are handy for stirring hot foods as they don't conduct heat in the way that metal spoons do. Also, they won't scratch delicate surfaces on pans.

Index